THE ACADEMIC MYSTERYHOUSE

the man, the campus, and their new search for meaning

ROBERT MERRILL HOLMES

Nashville   ABINGDO N PRESS   New York

THE ACADEMIC MYSTERYHOUSE

Copyright © 1970 by Abingdon Press

ISBN 0-687-00693-7

Library of Congress Catalog Card Number: 73-124758

SET UP, PRINTED, AND BOUND BY
THE PARTHENON PRESS, AT NASHVILLE,
TENNESSEE, UNITED STATES OF AMERICA

In the memory of
my father
Merrill J. Holmes,
his father
Edmund M. Holmes,
and my father-in-law
E. Leigh Mudge
educators and ministers in Jesus Christ

FOREWORD

"Nothing," said T. M. Cornfield of Cambridge, "should ever be done for the first time." It is increasingly apparent, however, that in the decade into which we have now moved, more and more things are to be done for the first time. The old molds are largely broken and former blueprints are no longer adequate. Heretofore commonly accepted living patterns are being questioned and many traditional answers to current issues are being rejected. All this adds up to make living infinitely harder and infinitely more exciting.

That the times should change so much is not a universally shared judgment, however. While there are those who feel quite strongly that the eighth decade of the century calls for new patterns of thinking, new modes of behavior, and new structures of society, there are others who feel equally strongly that the need is to recapture something that has been lost out of the past, to return to—or perhaps simply hold on to—certain values, systems, and procedures as we and our grandparents have known them.

This describes the fundamental tension that has marked our society in our time. It is a tension that has rapidly taken on the character of a civil war, the sides being drawn ideologically rather than geographically. To characterize it as simply a generation gap is too facile. It is rather a gap between those whose focus of attention is upon a new world coming and those whose focus is upon some golden age lost, and the ages are mixed on both sides. To distinguish the two sides, as did the late Bishop James Pike, as "the open and the uptight" is to prejudice the case. But it may be fair, at the risk of oversimplification, to identify them as those who seek to preserve order and tradition even at the expense of humanness, as contrasted with those who seek to enhance humanness even at the expense of order and tradition.

In the center of this tension is set the contemporary university, pushed and pulled from within and without by both kinds of forces, struggling not just for survival but for identity, seeking to unravel the compounding mysteries of our time in the light of an accelerating fund of knowledge and in the face of earnest, sometimes bitter, criticisms by increasing numbers who speak of the irrelevance, disenchantment, and meaninglessness of college education. In confronting these challenges, much that the university is called upon to do may well have to be done for the first time.

If the situation were hopeless, there would scarcely be a point in reading a book about it, let alone writing one. Hopelessness is by no means the mood of these pages. But if hopelessness is not, urgency is. The issues before our society, and thus before our universities, must now be met with accelerating speed, though not at the expense of penetrating depth. It is a task that calls for the best of the combined efforts of those on both sides of thirty, both ends of the log, and both sides of the campus boundary.

That is why this book is written with many publics in mind. I intend that my audience should be not only the professional educators who man the classrooms and administrative offices of our campuses, but also the laymen who serve as regents and trustees, with whom resides so much power in higher education and who yearn, in many instances, to understand more clearly where higher education is going and ought to go. As significant as any other part of my audience, it is hoped, will be those students in growing numbers who are taking society and its needs seriously to a degree not before witnessed in our nation, and who stand to be a profoundly important part not just of the *future* of our country, but the *present* of our universities. There is also that larger circle of people, lay and professional, who do not live and move and have their being on campuses, but who care very much what is happening and are in a position to provide the critically needed moral and financial support upon which our colleges and universities of every affiliation will always depend.

For all these publics this book was written in an effort to

sharpen certain issues and propose certain answers. If these pages serve to stimulate response in terms both of thoughtful discussion and positive action, the effort involved in its writing shall have been more than worth it.

Its writing (speaking of doing things for the first time) has been a trying and thrilling personal adventure. It began with the preparation of a doctoral dissertation some years ago under the instructive supervision of Dr. Charles S. McCoy and Dr. Robert Leslie, and ended with a much different kind of manuscript evolving out of my experience as the chaplain of a college that is typical in the challenges it faces, the visions it holds, and the possibilities it embraces.

For assisting this venture to its completion, many are to be thanked, including students and others who, knowing of this project, encouraged, prodded, cajoled, and otherwise motivated the writer. Particular appreciation is felt for my colleague Dr. Thomas Dicken for perceptive comments on many parts of the manuscript, for Mrs. Harriet Popowski who brought to the proofs of this book the careful Seymour eye for accuracy and style, and most especially to Polly, my wife, who graciously combined, among others, the skills of writing instructor, typist, editor, therapist, and comrade.

RMH
Billings, Montana
May 4, 1970

CONTENTS

INTRODUCTION

From one perspective, the university is in better shape than ever before in history. Enrollments keep swelling, faculty salaries keep climbing, and the larger society—including the government—grows increasingly concerned, even if not always well informed, about the problems of higher education. Libraries are bigger, dormitories richer, and endowments fatter than ever before. It may be doubtful that the university's impact upon the larger culture has increased commensurately; nevertheless fewer colleges are scraping the bottom for financial support, and almost none of them want for public attention these days.

At the same time, campuses have not been so troubled for many years. There is grumbling in the faculty lounges, a rapid turnover in presidents' offices, and the students in steadily growing numbers are leaving far behind their former image as the beat and silent generation.

The situation is, to say the least, paradoxical. We are living in an age in which man is making ever bolder explorations into outer space while having made only the barest inroads into inner space. We live in a world in which man's highest aspirations for world communion are matched by epidemics of social cruelty and racial vengeance hardly becoming to prehistoric man. We are living in a nation which claims the choicest freedoms, the strongest defenses, and the highest standard of living in history, yet which is singularly devoid of any clear-cut national purpose.

We have become remarkably adept at dealing with things, from tiny transistors to massive moon rockets. Yet we find ourselves increasingly inept at dealing with persons—across an ocean, across town, or across the breakfast table. We have made significant progress in defeating disease and poverty

and certain natural enemies. Our biggest trouble continues
to be with people. Psychologists maintain that the trouble
people have with other people is usually rooted in the trouble
they have with themselves. Theologians press further to say
that the difficulty man has with himself and with others derives from a fundamental frustration in his relationship with
God.

In any event, all this presents a very disturbing picture for
education, which has specialized through the years in the
propagation and dissemination of truth and the sharpening
of the tools for the discernment of truth, ostensibly that the
truth might make men free. Educators have sought to develop
philosophies and techniques of education which would lend
themselves to the effective achievement of these tasks. We
hardly need more evidence than we presently have to per-
suade us that such aims have fallen far short of satisfactory
fulfillment. The truth has not made us free.

For example, what Masters and Johnson and others have
discovered about the sexual life of *homo sapiens* and the
incorporation of these discoveries into our formal and informal educational programs may be said to have freed man
from certain areas of ignorance, certain forms of self-decep-
tion, and certain kinds of guilt feelings, but the newfound
"freedoms" thus derived scarcely spell the sort of liberated
condition which truth is supposed to bring. The perfection of
the revolutionary formula $e=mc^2$ has freed man from the
bonds of pre-Einsteinian conceptualizations and opened the
way to unparalleled achievements in the physical realm, but
such radical reformations concurrently threaten him with
new chances for annihilation. Neither the revision of the
physics curriculum nor the round-the-clock endeavors of the
radiation laboratories have markedly reduced this possibility.
Medical science has done much to lengthen man's life and
make it more comfortable, but it has not done much to make
his life more meaningful.

The most recent chapters of the modern industrial revolution have enabled man, both on the job and at home, to ac-
complish more in fewer hours, only to leave him with the

problem of what to do with the time thus saved—an issue which has yet to receive more than "extracurricular" attention in our programs of education. Whereas the accumulation of factual information about man and his world is accelerating by geometric progression, there is no evidence that man's understanding of the meaning of life in this world has deepened appreciably. In fact there is a general complaint that the reverse is true. To many, life seems to have less meaning than it ever had before. At any rate, modern man, to whom are available unprecedented quantities of data concerning himself and his world, is not at all sure who he is and where he is going. Notwithstanding many newspaper mastheads and library archways which display only half of an indivisible scriptural dictum, truth has *not* made men free.

Contemporary education, in the midst of this milieu, suffers from ambiguities of self-understanding and uncertainties of direction unparalleled in history. Its unprecedented expansion has come at a time when the mood of educational reform is at its height. It is to be expected that the anthropological uncertainties that obtain in our culture generally should find expression in vacillating philosophies of education, though it is pointless to identify either as the cause of the other. Rather, we must acknowledge that the university is a "microcosm of the macrocosm," a sample of the "fallen order" in which many of the ills of our culture as a whole are observable in particular detail.

Yet to absolve the university of blame, in this sense, is not to free it of responsibility, for it stands in a position of particular responsibility in and to our society. The university is clearly charged with the task of providing a forum in which the most intensive analysis of our time and culture may take place, and in which the most responsible efforts to cure its ills may be proposed. Its responsibility for *transmitting* and *transforming* culture is as mandatory as its function of *reflecting* culture is inevitable. We have every reason to expect the universities of our land to take the lead in shaping the future to a degree even more profound and far-reaching than our unprecedented technological development has led us. But how can the university fulfill its vital role when it is itself torn and confused by a welter of internal problems?

The university seems trapped in a vicious circle of which it is tacitly aware but from which it seems powerless to extricate itself. Conferences of faculty members, students, and administrators continue to be held periodically, and the summary reports that issue therefrom sound about the same every year. It is generally conceded that a pervasive sense of alienation has invaded the campus, a growing atmosphere of depersonalization, accelerated proliferation of both curriculum and community, and a keen awareness of the striking irrelevance of most of what is learned in college. It has been said that our universities do an excellent job of preparing us for the last century. Most assuredly, progress has been made in identifying the problems of the campus, but there has been little discernible headway toward their solution.

It is doubtful that another book on the subject of the dilemmas of higher education will be of much help unless it sheds some genuinely fresh light on these issues. We hardly need another page to tell us, for example, that (a) the central human search is for a sense of *meaning* in life, and that this quest is crucial in the life of the university, or that (b) there is a crying need for a more careful sense of *responsibility* on the part of individuals and institutions that are to direct the present and shape the future of our society. It may be—and this is the central contention of this book—that these very issues of meaning and responsibility about which so much has been written and so little done, are interrelated to an extent that requires their being dealt with conjunctively, and that the imprudence of trying to deal with them separately describes the folly of many efforts to solve the dilemmas of higher education.

One other fundamental relationship, frequently overlooked as inconsequential, provides the context for these chapters, and that is the mutual bearing of the problems of the collective university and the individual self upon each other. The problems of the contemporary Western university and those of the modern Western self are parallel, but more than this they are mutually contributive. Each adds to the problem of the other. If health is to be brought to our troubled selves and colleges, each must somehow lend to the healing of the other. The ills of our institutions of higher learning are not likely to be solved ultimately by detached theorists, eager politicians, or benevolent businessmen alone. Without in any way underrating the importance of the moral and financial support which must be increasingly forthcoming from the public at large, I submit that the problems of the universities will be dealt with most creatively by the selves who comprise them. Nor must the individuals who meet this challenge be administrators only. Solutions will require participation and some measure of sacrifice, perhaps even compromise on the part of all those who comprise academia, not the least of whom will be students. Trustees and regents stand to be among the most or the least helpful, depending upon the degree of genuine involvement they undertake in the struggles of all the components of the university. The day of campus control by a clique of biannual campus visitors is rapidly passing. This does not mean that trustees will be less important than before. On the contrary, it suggests that their active and informed participation is more important than ever before. But *participation* is the key word, and the kind of participation will be crucial.

Certainly there is nothing startling about the suggestion that the health of selves and their communities rise and fall together. Perhaps this is something which we have known in our heads, but the significance of which has not made its way to our hearts. In any event, there is no community today that more urgently requires a conscious reordering of goals on both the collective and individual levels than the American university. Every campus rings with cries of irrelevance, both curricular and extracurricular. Students are said to graduate from college with more knowledge and less meaning today than ever before. The irony of this charge resides in the fact that with the vast reservoir of intellect, talent, and creativity in the academic communities of our land, our colleges should be among the most timely, relevant, and crucial institutions in our society.

Though the word irrelevance has become passé, the phenomenon to which it refers, unfortunately, has not. If we are to deal with this issue, under whatever synonym we prefer to give it, we must, I shall contend, deal with it by way of finding meaning through responsibility.

It is this journey to meaning to which this volume is directed. Meaninglessness in higher education is fast becoming an area of crisis, and one that warrants not only more universal but more informed concern. The situation does not call for despair. If the prognosis were hopeless there would hardly be any point in reading about the problem, much less writing a book about it. Quite to the contrary, I approach this crisis with a sense of urgency matched by a commensurate attitude of hope. A small fraction of that hope is represented in the present volume, offered as an aid to those who are responsible for finding a route to the end of irrelevance on campus.

1

A college of liberal arts is partly high school, partly university, partly general, partly special. Frequently it looks like a teacher training institution, frequently it looks like nothing at all. And the degree it offers seems to certify that the student has passed an uneventful period without violating any local, state, or federal laws.

—Mayor John Lindsay

What . . . is a puddle? A puddle repeats infinity and is full of light; nevertheless, if analyzed objectively, a puddle is a piece of dirty water spread very thin on mud. The two great historic universities of England have all this large and level reflective brilliance. They repeat infinity. They are full of light. Nevertheless, or rather on the other hand, they are puddles. Puddles, puddles, puddles, puddles.

—G. K. Chesterton

We've all been brought up on *Tootle,* the children's tale in which baby locomotives are told to stay on the tracks no matter what. Don't go off to look at the buttercups, don't take short cuts to race with the stallions.

—David Shapiro
Columbia University Student

In San Jose, California, is one of the most remarkable houses in North America. Once the home of Mrs. Winchester, the widow of the famous rifle developer, the edifice is now called the Winchester mysteryhouse. Oral tradition tells us that in her later years Mrs. Winchester fell victim to certain paranoiac delusions, perhaps spurred on by a local soothsayer, who convinced her that her house was to be subject to the haunting activities of the spirits of the innocent

THE
ACADEMIC MYSTERYHOUSE

victims of Winchester rifles. She came to believe that her only defense against these demons was to continue perpetually building her house. She hired a full complement of carpenters, plumbers, bricklayers, and painters in order that the noise of their unceasing labors, added to the confusing outcome of their uncorrelated efforts, would confound the spirits.

Plagued by these delusions and financed by her almost limitless wealth, Mrs. Winchester built and built and built. The result is a monumental hodgepodge of building upon building, floor upon floor, room upon useless room. Crammed into dull, dark corners where their true beauty would never be discovered were the most elegant chandeliers, stained-glass windows, and inlaid wood floors, scarcely if ever seen by eyes other than her own. To compound the confusion, supporting posts were installed upside down, staircases were built to ceiling trapdoors which led nowhere, doors were hinged to open into blank walls, elevators ascended one floor to no exit, and stair steps of less than two inches elevation were constructed. Artists were engaged to paint cheap wood to look expensive, while beautiful woods were whitewashed. No expense was spared. All that was lacking was an overall design, for Mrs. Winchester was her own architect, and the house is a monument to her deranged mind. Once intended as a haven of blessing, the property is now only a tourist attraction, a curiosity which one may tour for a dollar and a half.

With all its combined humor and pathos, the Winchester house is the most pertinent image I have found of the contemporary university. The analogies hardly require amplification: The patternless growth, the busywork, the wasted artistry and talent, the phony facades, the fracture with the surrounding community—all lend themselves to a caricature of today's institutions of higher learning which have been variously characterized as both magnificent and sick. In this "academic mysteryhouse" we educators have not precisely identified the evil spirits we are hoping to foil by the complexity of our structures. Perhaps it is the ghost of eras past which threatens to return and haunt us. In any event, it is questionable whether the end result is a legitimately complex multiversity or a monument to schizophrenia. The predicament might be amusing if it weren't so pathetic.

The mysteryhouse image is equally applicable to the modern self, living in what has been variously called "the age of anxiety," "the era of alienation," and "a time of lost identity." Max Scheler suggests that "in approximately ten centuries of history, this is the first in which man finds himself completely and utterly 'problematical,' in which he no longer knows what he is and simultaneously knows that he does not have the answer." [1]

That our individual and corporate life is fractured by mass confusion and both emotional and social breakdown is not only a general anthropological observation; it is an intensely personal reality to which ample testimony has been given by contemporary art, drama, and literature, not to mention professional journalism. This is an era of greatly troubled selves who remain mysteries to themselves and to one another. And nowhere is this more evident than in the microcosms of our society, the beleaguered university campuses. It is a presupposition of this book that the emotional unrest of the individual and the apparent schizophrenia of the university are intimately related and must be both seen and solved conjunctively.

THE LOST DIMENSION IN EDUCATION

The Winchester mysteryhouse lacks an overall scheme. It is unclear to the tourist investigating the house what it's really all about. Again the image is apropos to both the university and the selves who comprise it. When one beholds the modern university, with all its proliferation of purpose and activity, he finds it hard to perceive what it's really all about. The situation on today's campus might be described by the impassioned words of a thoughtful Berkeley student who

---

[1] *Philosophical Perspectives* (Boston: Beacon Press, 1959), p. 65.

expressed his disenchantment with the university some months prior to the famous uprisings of 1964:

> We accede to dull classes, we take tests, we fill out forms, we regurgitate material; all of which holds close to no meaning for us. We embrace by deadly silence, and by ritualistic performance, a strikingly banal institution. The life of the university and college is all but a life of meaningless process. . . . It is possible to envisage all the youth of America under a bright banner, *We Demand Meaning.* . . . We have intense meaning in one area of our lives, in politics; now we must demand meaning in our education.[2]

An examination of student protests against university education, more or less articulate, more or less sophisticated, will doubtless reveal that the heart of the problem lies at this very point—the struggle against meaninglessness. A University of Illinois honor student put it this way: "You exist from one argument to the next, living for the next time the exam is over—only to start right in on the next one. The pace doesn't let you stop and take a look at *what* you're doing and *why.* That's how I managed to make the honor list—big deal! I don't even know why I care—or even *if* I care." [3] Similarly, a bitter M.I.T. senior is quoted as saying: "It's a rat-race, a grind, a meaningless ride on a rollercoaster. I'm just counting the days till it's over." [4]

The cry is not a new one. It is not essentially different from the cries heard twenty-five or fifty years ago. What is different is that what was once a muffled plea of an ignorable minority has become a rebel yell by a near majority. It is a cry which issues in varieties of action vastly different from the innocuous scholarly papers and debates that bored the majority of the collegiates of the panty-raid era. An analysis of British higher education made nearly forty years ago by Walter

---

[2] Brad Cleaveland in an unpublished manuscript, "The New Imperative: A Call for Radical Educational Reform."
[3] "Tormented Generation," *Saturday Evening Post,* October 12, 1963, p. 34.
[4] *Ibid.*

Kotschnig could hardly be more relevant to contemporary American higher learning:

> So far as their university students are concerned, most students are nowhere confronted with the challenge or opportunity to see life steadily and whole. They are not stimulated to regard their own lives as a whole rather than as a set of disconnected experiences, to make a plan of life and to feel responsibility for it, to face a life challenge and to make a life-choice. . . . In practice, of course, students must and do integrate their lives in some degree, but generally the university does not help them.[5]

It is this apparently perennial fact of American education that occasions such assertions as young Cleaveland's "we demand meaning in our education!" The entire drama of modern higher education is clouded over by a disturbing ambiguity: an increasing number of educators asserting that questions of meaning lie at the heart of the educative task, and at the same time the similarly growing accusations against the university for its failure to fulfill this responsibility. Somehow the central quest for a sense of meaning in life has failed to be anticipated or even reflected in the patterns and programs of higher education, and the cries of dismay are all the greater because of the age-old expectation that institutions of higher learning will be part of the answer instead of part of the problem.

Questions of life's meaning and destiny are, by definition, religious questions. Paul Tillich has called the plane on which these questions are raised the "dimension of depth" in human life. He asserts that even contemporary religion is beset by the loss of this dimension.[6] While religion, he says, has specialized in attending to man's personal and social needs on a horizontal plane, the vertical plane of man's honest confrontation with his predicament as a human being and of the deeper implications of his eternal relationship with the Divine has

---

[5] Walter Kotschnig and Elined Prys, *The University in a Changing World* (London: Oxford University Press, 1932), p. 11.

[6] "The Lost Dimension in Religion," *Adventures of the Mind*, ed. Richard Thruelsen and John Kohler (New York: Alfred A. Knopf, 1959), pp. 47-56.

been slighted. Yet it is this plane on which questions of ultimate meaning are raised that is the truly "religious dimension" in life.

By the same token it may be said that the inattention, or at
least insufficient attention, to the question of meaning in the
contemporary academic enterprise represents a lost dimension in education. While education has attended to man's
"horizontal" needs—the needs for knowledge, skills, certain
social abilities—what has been slighted is the most crucial
dimension of all: the vertical dimension, the dimension in
which not *what* a man does nor *how* he does it but *why* he
does it is raised, the dimension in which considerations of
meaning, purpose, and value are seriously undertaken. Tillich's judgment is that "in this country the public school
presumably on higher as well as secondary levels has ceased
to give an education which in any sense could be called initia-
tive into the mystery of existence and the symbols through
which it is expressed." [7] Elsewhere Tillich notes quite simply
and directly: "The spiritual disintegration of our day con-
sists in the loss of an ultimate meaning of life by the people of
Western civilization. And with the loss of an ultimate meaning of life they have lost personality and community." [8] The
quest for, and loss of, meaning is clearly both a personal and
collective problem with both psychological and sociological
implications; hence the validity—the necessity—of our insistence that the problems of the self and the university be
pursued conjunctively.

A useful starting point might be a brief look into the psychological history of contemporary man with a focus on this
lost dimension and a view to tracing implications for the university.

In 1940, Rollo May, noted psychiatrist, began his first book,
The Springs of Creative Living, with the sentence: "People
suffer personality breakdown because they do not have meaning in their lives" [9]—a thesis that serves as a working pre-

[7] *Theology of Culture* (New York: Oxford University Press, 1959), p. 151.
[8] *The Protestant Era* (Chicago: University of Chicago Press, 1948), p. 262.
[9] (New York and Nashville: Abingdon Cokesbury, 1940), p. 13.

supposition of his latest book, *Love and Will*.[10] In the ensuing years a number of psychologists have increased their attention to the importance of the human search for meaning. But no one to date has focused on this concern and its place in mental health as has the Viennese psychiatrist Viktor Frankl, who has oriented an entire therapeutic style around the question. A Jewish professor of neurology and psychiatry at the University of Vienna and director of the neurological and psychotherapeutic department of the Vienna Polyclinic, Frankl was a victim of Nazi tyranny during the Second World War. Over a two-and-a-half-year period he was interred in four concentration camps, including Auschwitz and Dachau, while his wife, his brother, and both parents lost their lives. Out of this experience, added to his many years of exploration in the field of psychiatry both before and after the war, his "existential analysis" of modern man evolved. Frankl's thought will be of special help to our pursuit of a key to the meaning problem.

Frankl's most frequent distinction between his own psychology and those of Freud and Adler revolves around motivational theory. While Freud conceives of man as driven primarily by the "will to pleasure," and Adler sees him as driven by the "will to power," Frankl asserts that even more fundamental is man's "will to meaning." This compulsion to discover meaning in life is an inward necessity occasioned by the very nature of the human species.

This inward necessity is not to be understood on the intellectual level and therefore cannot properly be called a "drive." It is more accurately a "pull" which derives from that within man which most nearly describes his humanness, his yearning to know why he was born. Rather than suggest that the will to pleasure or the will to power are erroneous formulations, Frankl asserts that these drives do indeed reside in man but are not dominant in him. Efforts to attain pleasure or power in hopes of finding ultimate meaning are inevitably futile. All such quests are merely ill-devised and

[10] (New York: W. W. Norton, 1969).

ill-fated attempts to find meaning, and they never succeed
in providing deep and lasting satisfaction. "Pleasure is an
effect of meaning fulfillment; power is a means to an end. A
degree of power—economic, for instance—is generally a
prerequisite of meaning fulfillment. But while the will to
pleasure mistakes the effect for the end, the will to power
mistakes the means to an end for the end itself." [11]

Psychoanalysis was not unaware of the will-to-meaning
phenomenon, but falsely identified it as pathological. "The
moment a man questions the meaning and value of life he is
sick," Freud wrote, "since objectively neither has any existence; by asking this question one is merely admitting to a
store of unsatisfied libido to which something else must have
happened, a kind of fermentation leading to sadness and
depression." [12]

Schooled initially in the Freudian tradition, Frankl soon
broke ties with this narrow doctrine and has since been wag-
ing the existentialist battle against any theory of man which
reduces him to something less than he really is, or which fails
to take into proper account man's whole nature and most
particularly those aspects of his nature from which his humanness actually derives.

THREE ENEMIES OF MAN AND HIS UNIVERSITIES

Every individual self is beset by three enemies. Frankl
identifies them as those conceptions of man which undercut
his essential humanness and prevent him from being man.
Frankl has declared open war against these misconceptions
in the interest of assisting man to be man. I am suggesting
that the same enemies confront the university and tend to
prevent it from being what it is called to be; therefore these
enemies should be clearly identified and challenged in the interest of assisting the university to be the university.

The first enemy is what Frankl calls *reductionism*, that

[11] "The Will to Meaning," *The Christian Century*, April 22, 1964, p. 515.
[12] Letter to Princess Bonaparte in *Letters of Sigmund Freud*, ed. Ernst
Freud (New York: Basic Books, 1960), p. 436.

view of man which takes seriously only one or two aspects of his nature and hence reduces man to nothing but those aspects. But man is much too complex a being for any reductionist view to be valid. Man is an enigma, often self-contradictory, and our intellectual history is strewn with the wreckage of anthropological oversimplifications. According to Frankl, Dynamic Psychology is particularly guilty at this point, for rather than simply illumining in a helpful and needed way those aspects of man which derive from his instincts and pleasure drives, it has oriented a total understanding of man around these forces, and its efforts to systematize and simplify an understanding of man on this basis have resulted in a grave distortion.

Frankl's contention is that the varied and apparently contradictory aspects of man's nature can best be understood dimensionally. Given to extensive use of metaphors and analogies, Frankl has used a number of figures to illustrate this point. One is that of a drinking glass. Here the figure of dimensionality is strikingly apropos. If one concentrates on one dimension of man's nature, ignoring the others, he will fail to understand man just as surely as one will fail to comprehend the real nature of a drinking glass by looking at its side or its bottom. The projected figures of a rectangle and a circle are as mutually contradictory as are the psychic and somatic natures of man, and all efforts to reconcile the two views are futile save as they are seen as legitimate and real dimensions of the same object in its unity and dimensionality. When they are so viewed, all false dichotomies between circle and rectangle (or body and mind) disappear, even though the real difference between the two dimensions remains apparent.

The drinking-glass figure, however, does not stop here; and this, Frankl contends, is where most psychological anthropology errs, for it does tend to stop with its two-dimensional psycho-somatic view of man. Yet just as there is more to the drinking glass than is immediately discernible in the projections of circle and rectangle, so there is something more to man than is detected either by stethoscope or on the psychiatrist's couch. And that "more" is not merely *another* dimension, but the *crucial* dimension for discovering the real nature of the entity in question. What is overlooked by the too-simple projections of side and end of the glass is the openness at one end which makes the glass a vessel and reveals the really essential nature of the glass. In the case of man, this dimension which is absent in the too-simple psycho-somatic conceptualization is the "spiritual" dimension for understanding the whole. Man is a spiritual being, and it is this spirituality, in fact, which marks his essential uniqueness among animals.

The word "spiritual" implies something of a mystical-religious nature which Frankl does not necessarily intend, and which is not inferred by the word *noetic*, which bears reference to objective values though not necessarily to deity. Frankl uses this word to mean "religion in the nonspecific sense."

It is not only by acknowledgment of, but by explicit attention to man's noetic or "noölogical" dimension that he is more fully viewed and his needs more accurately understood. It is in this dimension that man's religious needs and questions abide and must be taken seriously if man is to be taken seriously. Whether or not one speaks of these matters in the specifically religious terms of one's relationship to God, this is nevertheless the dimension in which questions of meaning and value are to be found and dare not be slighted. Yet this is the very dimension which is in constant danger of going largely unheeded, especially on the college campus.

The second enemy of the self, according to Frankl, is *pandeterminism*, which conceives of man as the pawn of a complex of forces within and outside his life which divest him of any real freedom and therefore of responsibility. Such a view lulls man into thinking he has no real power of decision whereas this power is, in fact, one of the essential characteristics which identify him as human! If man fails to exercise this freedom to make choices, he fails to fulfill his human being, for man is "the essence which always decides. And he again and again decides what he will be in the next instant." [13]

Frankl does not claim for man an unlimited freedom. No man who had languished in a Nazi concentration camp could make such a claim. Certain social, biological, and psychological factors may be strongly influential in changing the conditions of a man's life. But *though man's freedom is always limited, it is never eliminated.*

While man may have little control over what happens to him, he does have a large measure of control over what he does about what happens to him, which is to say how he *responds* to what happens to him. "Being human is being responsible because it is being free," [14] says Frankl. Conversely, one is free only insofar as he fulfills his freedom to respond, and to the measure that he fails to fulfill his responsibility he is not free and therefore not really human, for "existential analysis views being-responsive as the essence of human existence." [15]

Doctrines of man and theories of therapy which neglect this central fact are, according to Frankl, not only erroneous; they are insidious.

> There is a danger we may corrupt a man, that we may work into the hands of his nihilism and thus deepen his neurosis if we present him with a concept of man which is not the true concept of man; if we make a man into a homunculus. The modern homunculus is not produced in the alchemist's vaults . . . but wherever we present man as an automaton of reflexes, as a mind-machine or a bundle of instincts, as a pawn of drives and reactions, as a mere product of instinct, inheritance and environment.[16]

The third enemy of the self is what Frankl calls the *homeostasis theory,* which defines man's ideal state as one in which all tension and conflict are absent. Much therapy is

---

[13] *Logos und Existenz* (Wien: Verlag Franz Deutlicke, 1951), p. 7.

[14] *The Doctor and the Soul: An Introduction to Logotherapy,* trans. Richard and Clara Winston (New York: Alfred A. Knopf, 1955), p. 87.

[15] "Existential Analysis and Logotherapy," *Surgo* (Candlemas, 1960), p. 6.

[16] "The Concept of Man in Psychotherapy," *Pastoral Psychology,* November 1955, pp. 16-26.

directed toward this state of balanced tranquillity—homeostasis. This misdirection, says Frankl, encourages man to be
less than human. Though man may and should undertake to
relieve certain levels of tension in his life, underlying everything is a fundamental tension that is essential for his human
existence. This is the quest for meaning in life which, to say
the least, involves struggle, anxiety, uncertainty, and frustration. Man's need is not for homeostasis but for "noödynamics"
—a spiritual dynamic in a polar field of tension where the one
pole is represented by a meaning to be fulfilled and the other
by the man who has to fulfill it.[17] Frankl gives this essential
tension the impressive name "existential frustration," and
contends that failure to recognize this normal human phenomenon for what it is and make the best use of it results in
the human condition which he characterizes as "existential
vacuum"—the lack of a sense of meaning in life. And nature,
abhorring a vacuum in the psychological sphere of reality
quite as much as in the sphere of physics, rushes in with
spurious remedies to fill the emptiness—all manner of busy-
ness, addictions, artificial thrills, limited purposes, and ill-
placed commitments. But all such frantic efforts fail to obscure the central issue, which is man's frustrated quest for
meaning. Frankl contends that not only do we fail to understand who man really is until we acknowledge his quest for
meaning, but we will fail to meet his real need until we meet
him at the point of his existential frustration and help him to
provide an *authentic* occupant for his existential vacuum.

There are those whose ideal picture of the university is a
citadel of ivy-covered tranquillity where students attend to
their books, teachers attend to their students, and the administration attends to a well-endowed budget; where the pastoral atmosphere is interrupted only by an occasional spirited
ball game or lively academic debate. But there are others, and
I am one of them, who consider this kind of homeostasis to be

---

[17] "Basic Concepts of Logotherapy," *Journal of Existential Psychiatry,*
Spring 1962, pp. 111-18.

patently phony. Just as the self that is genuinely human will be acted upon by internal and external tensions, so the university that is worthy of its name will be characterized by repeated if not constant tensions and frustrations, internal and external, revolving primarily around the question of the meaning of its existence. This "existential frustration" is not to be bemoaned or ignored, but must be capitalized upon, taken with ultimate seriousness, viewed as crucial to the essential purpose of the university. The theory that views absence of tension as the ideal state for either the self or the university is, indeed, an enemy of both.

Here, then, are three enemies which provide deterrents to the human quest for meaning in life and which must be faced and dealt with if ever the lost dimension in the self or in education is to be recovered.

Frankl's theories carry more weight when we remember the brutal limitations under which he lived for many months. If anyone ever had reason to conclude that man is powerless to respond to the outside forces which determine his fate, and that in the last analysis life's ideal state would be tensionlessness, that person is a survivor of a Nazi concentration camp. Yet Frankl rejected these tempting theories. Frankl asserts that his "existential analysis" of man was not born in the death camp so much as it was borne out in the death camp. He would have us see that the experience at Auschwitz and elsewhere was merely a starkly dramatic capsulized version of the general human existential situation. Man, victim of fateful forces over which he has little or no absolute control, suffering not only physical pain and privation, but the anxiety of losing all those things which have heretofore made life worthwhile, confronting the certain eventuality of death, seeing the best of his creativity destroyed—this is man as he exists in the world, struggling against all those forces within and without, which would whittle away at his humanity and make him less than the self that he was meant to be. The search for meaning is, therefore, a pervasive human search, and what we have called the lost dimension in education is the lost dimension of life.

Surely this dimension is recoverable, but how? How can the university be expected to provide for its members a solution to a problem from which it suffers itself? Meaning is not, after all, something students may realistically "demand" of a university. No university should be expected to provide meaning along with its meals, books, and credit hours, packaged and dispensed according to the I.Q. of the student. Meaning cannot be given to faculty along with tenure. On the other hand, neither should the university continue to ignore or plead helplessness in the face of such a crucial deficiency.

We seem to be left with a dilemma, but not, I submit, an insoluble one. Its solution requires, paradoxically, both a serious *focus* on the problem of meaning and an appropriate *inattention* to it. That is to say the central ills of both the self and the university will not be dealt with properly apart from due attention to the quest that is critical to the unique existence of both; yet at the same time the "meaning of life" is one of those evasive realities of life that is not found by looking for it. The questions left us by this paradox provide the context of the subsequent chapters which, hopefully, will point the way to a solution of the meaning problem.

We must begin by bringing clarity to a serious confusion. The most problematic aspect of the question of meaning is the meaning of the question. What, after all, does one mean when he speaks of, searches for, and possibly discovers, "the meaning of life"? Let's begin there.

2

The concept of *meaning,* in all its varieties, is the dominant concept of our time.

—*S. Langer*[1]

Poland's top Marxist philosopher, Professor Adam Schaff, head of the philosophy department of the University of Warsaw, and a member of the Central Committee of the Polish Communist Party, reported a seminar in Warsaw in which a student asked simply: "Please don't be angry, but could you explain the meaning of life, Sir?" "I first thought," reports Schaff, " 'Is he baiting me?' But when I looked at the student and saw hundreds of pairs of eyes watching me attentively, I understood: This is serious. It was confirmed by the silence with which my explanations were followed. I admit that I was thinking out loud, and very feverishly. Until then I had rejected such subjects as so much blah-blah."

—*Time*[2]

This most profound and elusive of all questions is by no means a distinctly American nor a uniquely twentieth-century one. It is a human question which has been brought to bear with particular intensity upon the present century. But while it is unquestionably in vogue now to raise the question of meaning and to bemoan its absence, there is anything but a concensus as to what anyone is talking about when he speaks of "the meaning of life." L. Jonathan Cohen has spoken of the "notorious obscurity of the word, 'meaning,' "[3] and the two Oxford philosophers C. K. Ogden and I. A. Richards, in

---

[1] *Philosophical Sketches* (Baltimore: Johns Hopkins Press, 1962), p. 55.
[2] June 2, 1961, p. 61.
[3] *The Diversity of Meaning* (New York: Herder & Herder, 1963), p. 24.

FOUR MEANINGS OF MEANING

their classic work on *The Meaning of Meaning*, have noted
that "a study of the utterances of philosophers [they might
have added educators] suggests that they are not to be trusted
in their dealings with meaning." [4]

An example of such imprecise utterances might be a statement of E. Z. Friedenberg in *Coming of Age in America:*[5]
"The highest function of education is to help people understand the meaning of their lives and become more sensitive to
the meaning of other people's lives and relate to them more
fully." In a sense this says everything there is to be said, yet
if the meaning of "the meaning of lives" is not clarified, this
sentence says almost nothing. Similarly, Huston Smith observes in *Condemned to Meaning*[6] that "teachers can help
with the problem of meaning both by exemplifying its presence in their lives and by seeing that the meaning-import of
their subject matter is not neglected." Yet even after drawing
several philosophical distinctions between kinds of meaning,
he stops short of being concrete as to what it means to exemplify the presence of meaning in one's life or how to identify
the "meaning-import" of a given subject. On still another
level Paul Denise, sharing "Some Thoughts Resulting from
the Disjuncture of Relevance at Berkeley," observes that
"the students were pressing for a basic redefinition of the
very meaning of the university which was not only unac-
ceptable but which was, I believe, genuinely incomprehensible
to most of its staff." [7] Indeed, the phrase "the meaning of the
university" remains incomprehensible to all of us unless it is
given more specific content.

Hence, the need confronts us to spell out with greater precision and a minimum of philosophical abstraction, what is
meant by this "notoriously obscure" word, *meaning,* which
we have called "the lost dimension in education." Unless we
are to do as Humpty Dumpty did in *Alice in Wonderland* and

---

[4] London: Routledge and Kegan, 1960), p. 185 (original copyright 1923).
[5] (New York: Random House, 1965).
[6] (New York: Harper & Row, 1965).
[7] "The Prophetic Microcosm and the Paracurriculum," *Yankee Student Opinion,* February 1965 (Cambridge: SCM in New England), p. 4.

let a word mean what we want it to mean, we shall have to
begin our investigation with a more careful delineation of
just what this lost dimension, in either the self or the university, entails.

The Ogden and Richards study just mentioned, though
written sometime ago, provides perhaps the most comprehensive single volume on the subject and the most useful base
from which to begin our own exploration of *the meaning of
meaning.* So varied are the uses to which this equivocal word
has been put by philosophers, scientists, psychologists, poets,
and educators, that the authors of this volume identify no
less than sixteen separate categories of definition. Of these,
four are immediately relevant to the problem of *the lost
dimension.* They are, as the authors give them:[8]

1. A unique unanalyzable relation to other things
2. The other words annexed to a word in the dictionary
3. An event intended or a volition
4. The place of anything in a system

Closely related to the fourth, and one that we shall include
with it for purposes of this book, is yet another category of
meaning:

5. The practical consequences of a thing in our future
   experience.

The distinguishing of even these few meanings of meaning
is sufficient to illustrate that to inquire as to the meaning of
life is to ask more than one question, and that a responsible
dealing with the question of the "meaning of life" demands
attention to the differing levels of the question inferred. We
will speak, then, of four *modes* of the question of meaning
which will need to be understood clearly and explored with
respect to both the self and the university if that which is lost
is ever to be found. Otherwise the most profound articulations about meaning will leave us in the ambiguous stew
in which we have always found ourselves, whose final con-

---

[8] *The Meaning of Meaning,* pp. 186-87. (The numbers here do not corre-
spond to those assigned by the authors. Not included here are those dealing
with categories of traditional logic, critical realism in philosophy, or signs
and symbols.)

clusion can only be that meaning is meaning is meaning. What follows is not as heady as it may appear. It is not an excursus into philosophical speculation. Behind the formidable terminology is an effort to spell out life's most profound questions in everyday terms, to provide handles for approaching the critical problem of meaning in an age threatened by meaninglessness. Hopefully these handles, specified in terms of four major quests, will be found helpful to the individual self and the university alike.

MEANING AND THE QUEST FOR WHOLENESS

Experience comes in small pieces. One of life's principal challenges is that of fitting the pieces together into a meaningful whole. On the first level, the problem of meaning expresses itself in this frustrating quest for a fundamental sense of the unity of knowledge and experience. I shall refer to this mode of the quest for meaning as the *phenomenological* mode. Phenomenology has been a name for several disciplines and an expression for various concepts, but throughout all these is the note of subjective experience. What is implied in my usage is that the variety of one's experience—physical, emotional, social, psychological, and intellectual—cry out for a sense of overall unity; that all the phenomena of one's experience, including not only what one does but what one encounters with the mind, call for unity. One wants to know not only how the social and physical experiences of his days fall into a meaningful pattern, but how the things learned in a course of study (that is, the things subjectively experienced by the mind) fit with life and with other things learned in other courses. While philosophy may speculate on the unity of *ultimate reality,* the phenomenological aspect of the meaning question seeks a unity of one's individual, total *experience of reality.*

Ogden and Richards have denoted this level of meaning as "a unique unanalyzable relation to other things." It concerns the manner in which things fit together. To ask, on this level, "What is the meaning of life?" is to ask, "How do all things fit together?"—not only, "How do all branches of knowledge and learning form a unified and comprehensible whole?" but, "How do the varieties and complexities of experience in life hold together in any kind of discernible pattern?" As Wilhelm Dilthey has concluded, meaning "is the comprehensive category through which life becomes comprehensible." [9]

To ask, "What is the meaning of *my* life?" in this context is to ask, "How do I fit in with all else that is in nature and in history? What is my relationship to what is?" To ask the meaning of any particular experienced object or event or piece of learning is to inquire how it fits into the total scheme of things. Harry Overstreet observes in *The Mature Mind* [10] that man is a creature that lives by and through relationships. His mind matures as he discovers the relation of objects and events to the tree of meaning. To fail to discern the relationship among things is one thing he means by *immaturity*. This, then, is the phenomenological aspect of the meaning question —the quest for integrity throughout all experienced phenomena of life.

While the fragmentation of experience is a phenomenon equally commom to student and professor, housewife and businessman, there may be no time in life in which this frustration is felt so keenly as in the teen and college years. Here one is exposed to all forms of new experience, a variety of disciplines, and new modes of thought, all in the midst of a felt need to make many of life's most important and far-reaching decisions concerning vocation, philosophy of life, and marriage partner. Hence it may be during these years more than any other that the sense of meaning, in terms of a quest for unity, is more urgently sought.

That this quest is in some sense a necessity for human life (and thus for education) has been attested by philosophers and psychologists alike. Karl Jaspers, in *The Idea of the University*, discusses it on the level of philosophical inquiry when he speaks of the needs of modern science:

[9] *Pattern and Meaning in History: Thoughts on History and Society,* ed. H. P. Richman (New York: Harper Torchbooks, 1962).
[10] (New York: W. W. Norton, 1949).

Propelled as it is by our primary thirst for knowledge, this
search is guided by our vision of the oneness of reality. We
strive to know particular data, not in and for themselves, but
as the only way of getting at that oneness. Without reference to
the whole of being science loses its meaning. With it, on the
other hand, even the most specialized branches of science are
meaningful and alive.[11]

To be sure, he goes on to say, we must acknowledge "the
fragmentary character of all knowledge," and in a real sense
the assigned task of any specialized science is such that it
"destroys my rapture at the beauty and harmony of the
world." Yet beneath and beyond this plurality I must become
aware of "the unity transcending and secretly motivating my
entire search for knowledge. Only this unity gives life and
meaning to my search." [12]

That the curriculum of the contemporary university bears
witness to the plurality of knowledge, there is little question.
That the university similarly bears witness to a fundamental
sense of unity underlying this plurality, there is considerable
doubt, for it is at this point of the increasingly fragmented
curriculum that a keen frustration is felt by faculty and students alike. As Whitehead once observed, the list of subjects
currently taught at the average university "is a rapid table of
contents which a deity might run over in his mind while he
was thinking of creating a world, and had not yet determined
how to put it together." [13]

The problem is not a new one. It is the very problem with
which John Cardinal Newman wrestled when he observed a
century ago the need for some sort of unifying principle above
and beyond the individual sciences—a task he proposed to
assign to theology.[14] In fact, the problem is as old as the days
of the confluence of Egyptian, Babylonian, and Phoenician
cultures and their respective specialization of knowledge and

[11] (Boston: Beacon Press, 1959), p. 21.
[12] *Ibid.*
[13] Alfred North Whitehead, quoted in Mark Van Doren, *Liberal Education*
(New York: Henry Holt, 1943), p. 114.
[14] *The Idea of a University* (Garden City, N.Y.: Doubleday & Co., Image
Book, 1959; first published 1852), chaps. iii and iv, esp. pp. 84-87.

experience. The quest for some sort of intellectual synthesis fed the roots of modern institutions of higher learning in the Academy and the Lyceum. Correlation became a major concern of the scholastics of the medieval universities and the French Encyclopedists, and in the nineteenth century, Hegel, Marx, and Darwin were driven by the same urge. But the need for synthesis has become more and more acute with the ever-accelerating accumulation of knowledge.[15]

By virtue of its very name, the university announces its concern with the unity of knowledge. Clark Kerr, former president of the University of California, asserts that the fact of increasing fragmentation is a characteristic of the modern world which must be acknowledged and accepted rather than bemoaned. Therefore he speaks of the *multiversity* as the "really modern university"—not a single community but several communities, the boundaries of which are indistinct, in appropriate consistency with the surrounding society.[16] There is some fear that Kerr's concept marks a dangerous acquiescence to fragmentation,[17] but Kerr maintains it is a simple acknowledgment of a fact of contemporary life. In any event, the need for unity of knowledge is more obvious in a "multiversity" than it ever was in less complex institutions.

This problem of lack of unity expresses itself on the contemporary scene in a number of ways, not the least of which is a notorious absence of communication among the faculty across departmental lines (and sometimes even within departments). One writer has said:

> Nine-tenths of the faculty at any university are bores simply because they become complete nincompoops outside their specialties. Most of them take their coffee breaks with their own

---

[15] A helpful discussion of the history of this problem is provided by Ernest Becker in Part I of his book *Beyond Alienation* (New York: George Braziller, 1967), pp. 3-86.

[16] *The Uses of the University* (Cambridge: Harvard University Press, 1963), pp. 6 and 45.

[17] See, e.g., "Whither the University?" (William Sheldon's review of Kerr's book), *Saturday Review*, November 1963, pp. 80 ff.

colleagues in order to avoid the viruses of other disciplines. They are not happy until their undergraduate majors become as narrow as they are themselves.[18]

The faculty has been trapped into manifesting and accentuating the very problem they are in part commissioned to help solve, and the university continues to be, as Archbishop Temple described it, "a place where a multitude of studies are conducted, with no relation between them except those of simultaneity and juxtaposition."[19]

Not only is there manifest absence of integration among the various courses of study within the curriculum, but there is an even more striking absence of relationship between what is learned and what is lived or experienced in the outside world of the present and the future. It is this disparity that was decried two decades ago by the *Report of the President's Commission*—that the student is too often " 'educated' in that he has acquired competence in some particular occupation, yet falls short of that human wholeness and civic consciousness which the cooperative activities of citizenship require."[20] What was once the subject of dispassionate analytic reports increasingly has become that of passionate student complaints. The almost desperate plea one hears time and time and time again is the cry for "relevance," which means *relatedness-to-life*.

At times it would almost appear that explicit efforts are made to obscure the practical implications of what is learned for what is to be lived. A student, addressing an audience of college and university administrators, noted:

[18] Claude Coleman, quoted by Robert Hutchins in "An Appraisal of American Higher Education," *A Century of Higher Education: Classical Citadel to Collegiate Colossus,* ed. William Brickman and Stanley Kehrer (New York: Society for the Advancement of Education, 1962), p. 202.

[19] In a sermon entitled "Freedom, Peace and Truth," preached before the University of Oxford, quoted in Sir Walter Moberly, *The Crisis in the University* (London: SCM Press, 1949), pp. 58-59.

[20] *Higher Education for American Democracy: A Report of the President's Commission on Higher Education* (Washington: U.S. Govt. Printing Office, 1947), p. 48.

The student who seeks practical insight into personal and public issues is frequently cautioned against any attempt to connect his classroom experience to life experience. Political scientists go to great lengths to make their students understand that their courses have nothing to do with practical politics. Introductory psychology lectures most frequently start with the caution that it is a dangerous thing to go around attempting to apply concepts learned about neurosis and such. And then, of course, the lecture goes on to discuss the nervous system of the rat.[21]

Little wonder that Michael Novak says, "It is even common for a student to go to class after class in sociology, economics, psychology . . . and the rest, and hardly become aware that he is dealing with issues of life and death, of love and solitude, of inner growth and pain." [22]

In writing of the importance of developing curriculum with regard for the theory of personality, Joseph Katz and Nevitt Sanford assert that "a student ought to have the experience, at least in one period of his development, of a passionate devotion to an overall religious or philosophical scheme which seems to him to explain everything." [23] This calls for a role on the part of the teacher that far outreaches the narrow provincialisms of departmental self-centeredness.

It should not be concluded, however, that mere efforts toward course integration are sufficient to meet the problem at hand. A variety of programs of integrated study have already evolved in response to this very need for wholeness, and general education itself has been an effort to meet the problem. It is possible to effect a measure of interdepartmental collaboration and synthesis and still fail to come to terms with

[21] Paul Potter, "The New Radical Encounters the University," *The Aim of Higher Education: Social Adjustment or Human Liberation?* ed. Ronald Barnes (St. Louis, Mo.: United Ministries in Higher Education, United Campus Christian Fellowship Publications Office, 1966).

[22] "God in Colleges," *Harper's,* October 1961, p. 174.

[23] "The Curriculum in the Perspective of the Theory of Personality Development," *The American College—A Psychological and Social Interpretation of the Higher Learning,* ed. Nevitt Sanford (New York: John Wiley & Sons, 1962), p. 435.

the deeper implications of wholeness. Moreover, integration of courses may approach this level of the meaning problem without beginning to deal with the other three levels yet to be discussed. [24]

What is needed is not so much that sense of unity which derives from a dogmatically and authoritatively imposed world view, but rather a growing intellectual and psychological state which might simply be called the "feeling of meaningfulness," the sense that the various academic and experiential "pieces" of creation's puzzle hold together, or at least are meant to, and that fitting into this puzzle somewhere is one's own self, complete with whatever interests and talents and potentials attend the self.

Here, then, is one aspect of the meaning problem—that which concerns the "meaningful wholeness" of creation. It concerns a need that is both communal and personal in nature; that is to say, the need for coherence is a need of the university as a community as well as of the persons who comprise it. This level of meaning is threatened on the contemporary campus not only by the persistent fragmentation of a curriculum or by a lack of effort to synthesize or integrate knowledge, or to relate learning to life, but by the resulting implication of a fragmented universe and of a world devoid of a sense of genuine community and personal integrity. This age calls for something more significant than the provision of interdisciplinary course studies or expanded personal counseling programs. It demands an approach that will be broader and more profound than this. It is precisely for this reason that so many superficially adventurous efforts at curricular reform have fallen so far short of solving the problem of the lost dimension, in both the individual and the university, a problem which will ultimately require simultaneous attention to all the modes of the meaning question.

[24] See David Riesman's discussion of the mixed effect of integration programs—how, for example, increased communication and fluidity within the groups so integrated can result in lessened communication outside them. (*Constraint and Variety in American Education* [Garden City: Doubleday & Co., 1958], pp. 83-99.)

MEANING AND THE QUEST FOR IDENTITY

The impossibility of any ultimate separation of these four levels of meaning will become increasingly apparent as we observe how the respective questions raised overlap one another and how the illustrations selected refuse to fit exclusively into one category of question. Our discussion thus far has implied a relationship between academic coherence and personal integration. The inference has been that the university member's intellectual and psychological needs are not ultimately separable, nor are the educational and therapeutic tasks of the university unrelated.

The second concept of the meaning question involves the quest for definition. Ogden and Richards have phrased this category almost humorously: "the other words annexed to a word in the dictionary." To ask, "What is the meaning of life?" on this level is to inquire, broadly, "How is life defined?" or, somewhat more specifically, "What is human life?"

While the question can be formulated on this general or anthropological level, it must ultimately become more personal: "How is my life defined?" Behind "What is man?" lies "Who am I?" What is sought on this level is a *personal definition,* an expression whose awkwardness turns us to the more familiar and outworn term, "identity." This is the question that deals with one's very *being;* hence it may be called the *ontological* level of meaning.

While the word "ontological" is normally employed as a philosophical term referring to that having to do with the theory of being *qua* being, in its usage here it has specifically to do with one's being as a person. Frankl employs the term in speaking of the "dimensional ontology" of the individual— that one's being is not only to be understood as psychological and physical, but three-dimensional: psychic, somatic, and noetic simultaneously. I have linked the term "ontology" with "identity," a word meaning one's personal definition, one's distinct being, if you please. It is on this level of the meaning question that psychology and education come into closest proximity.

Erik Erikson's analysis is helpful at this point, for he sees the loss of identity as a fundamental problem in the present day. "The study of identity, then, becomes as strategic in our time as the study of sexuality was in Freud's time." [25] Erikson has asserted that each stage of human growth is characterized by certain specific emotional disturbances which, although subject to differential diagnosis, are essentially determined by the life tasks of that stage. Each of these disturbances, if recognized as a normal crisis of inner growth, may be dealt with so as to prevent its becoming chronic. Each of these is most easily ameliorated during the very period of its emergence.

I have called the major crisis of adolescence the *identity crisis;* it occurs in that period of the life cycle when each youth must forge for himself some central perspective and direction, some working unity, out of the effective remnants of his childhood and the hopes of his anticipated adulthood; he must detect some meaningful resemblance between what he has come to see in himself and what his sharpened awareness tells him others judge and expect him to be.[26]

As this identity crisis extends beyond the high school years, Erikson speaks of it as the "post-adolescent crisis," particularly evident among freshmen and sophomores.[27] It would appear that the quest for identity is not only a part of the normal life process, but is an issue that comes to a head in the collegiate years.

The alternative to the establishment of a sense of identity is the development of what Erikson calls *identity-diffusion* which expresses itself in a purposelessness and an unwilling-

[25] *Childhood and Society* (New York: W. W. Norton, 1950), p. 242. See pp. 237-83 and 367-80.

[26] *Young Man Luther, A Study in Psychoanalysis and History* (New York: W. W. Norton, 1958), p. 14.

[27] *Identity and the Life Cycle* (New York: International University Press, 1959).

ness to be productive or to become involved. It seems generally agreed that the preoccupation with questions of personal
import has been accompanied historically by a minimal concern for the larger issues of society and the world. This is
precisely the condition that predominated among American
college students after World War II—a rise of individualistic
concern or "privatism," to which the pejorative synonym
"apathy" was applied—an apparent willingness to let the rest
of the world go by. Riesman described it as

> a preoccupation with private life, with human relations rather
> than international relations. Thus while some students enter
> anthropology or sociology who would have once gone into
> law, politics, or economics—that is, to better the world or their
> social position in it—many others enter the more social sciences
> in order to better their understanding of themselves.[28]

The most notable recent expression of this kind of withdrawal from social reality is the "drop out, tune in, turn on"
drug culture. This subculture is admittedly easy to oversim-
plify, nevertheless there is a sense in which the drug dropout
(not to be confused necessarily with the college dropout) expresses a new kind of apathy; "tuning in" becomes the latest
popular fad, and "turning on" becomes a fresh manifestation
of privatism. This kind of retreat from profound social involvement is one of two understandable but regrettable consequences of the continued frustration of student efforts to
gain some control over their own destiny. The other is the
opposite extreme—violence, which may either express hostile
desperation or become a kind of political strategy born of
complete disenchantment with the system and its built-in
procedures for change.

To be sure, during the sixties, there was a healthy increase
in student interest and activity in a broad range of issues,
from civil rights and foreign policy to the restructuring of
higher education itself. The students of the sixties exposed a
different profile than had been evident a decade earlier. While

[28] *Constraint and Variety in American Education*, p. 78.

more will be said of this later, two observations seem in order
at this point:

First, it is altogether too tempting to pose the thoughtfully
vocal and responsibly protesting student as typical of the current student generation. Such is by no means the case. While
such students constitute a steadily growing minority, they
remain a minority nonetheless. According to Elmira Ken-
dricks, former president of the National Student Christian
Federation, "The majority of students on U.S. campuses
during the 1960's cannot be easily distinguished from students
of the 1950's, or even the 1940's. They are, for the most part,
concerned about dates, athletic victories, grades and the like."
It takes, of course, only a committed minority to alter the
shape of history, and there is little doubt that today's growing
student minority has begun to do just this. The early months
of the 1970's disclosed a marked increase in both the extent
and the quality of the political involvement of college youth
with a renewed effort to "work within the system," even
including mounting pressure to dismiss classes to permit
maximum participation on political campaigns. Yet one dares
not overlook the collegiate majority of whom the aforemen-
tioned judgments are still valid—the remainder of the "silent
generation" who are still silent and largely inactive with
respect to world issues, being engaged in more private
pursuits.

Second, the current increase in social concern does not
necessarily imply a diminution of the importance of the personal quest for identity as a mode of the quest for meaning.
Quite the contrary, the growing tendency toward activism is
a specific expression of the quest for identity. It derives from
the much-discussed condition of "alienation" from which our
culture in general and youth in particular seems to suffer.
Sensitive students report a felt lack of control over the conditions of their lives in the university, much as Marx spoke of
the industrial man's loss of control over the instruments of
production in his day. This sense of alienation heightens the
question of identity. "If I am not one who helps to shape the

immediate environment—in this case the university in which I live and move and have my being—then who am I?"

Directly related to this feeling of nonparticipation in the adult world is youth's rejection of the ready-made identity which adults have previsioned and stored up awaiting his adoption. Leonard Blumberg notes the part which the "rejection of 'middle class adulthood' " plays in the collegian's lack of identity:

> The search for new meanings has involved a tendency to the idealization of the downtrodden, and the identification with the representatives of the downtrodden who are also participants in the nonviolent non-cooperative direct action. Insofar as this new basis of identification is Negro, and the student protestors are white, we may speak of a "universalization of the self." That is, in the general personality development of white American students, heretofore, there has been implicit an exclusion of Negroes. In part the whites defined themselves in apposition to Negroes. Under the new conditions, however, Negroes and whites are both included in the definition of what is an *American* student. The result is a more comprehensive, or more nearly universally human, way of looking at oneself.[29]

Hence both privatism and social activism must be viewed within the context of this mode of the search for meaning— the quest for identity.

This problem of identity, as it relates particularly to American women of our time, is the central theme of Betty Friedan's now famous book, *The Feminine Mystique*.[30] Mrs. Friedan introduces "the problem that has no name" by observing that beneath the surface of a general and growing unrest among countless American women is "a strange stirring, a sense of dissatisfaction, a yearning" that is deeper than a quest for sexual fulfillment, marriage, or even motherhood. Mrs. Friedan seems to support the contention that the

[29] "American Student Dissent in the Mid-Sixties" in *The Aim of Higher Education: Social Adjustment or Human Liberation,* ed. Ronald Barnes (St. Louis: United Christian Campus Foundation Publications, 1966), p. 20.

[30] (New York: W. W. Norton, 1963; also available in Dell paperback, 1964).

modern woman has been unknowingly sold "the pretty lie"
that the role for which she is properly destined is that of
wife and mother, and that divergence from this role is a
deviation from normality and, especially, from femininity.
This prevailing mystique permits and even encourages women
to ignore the question of their identity, conditioning them to be
content to define themselves exclusively in terms of their
relationship to their husbands and children. "It is my thesis,"
she says, "that as the Victorian culture did not permit women
to accept or gratify their basic sexual needs, our culture does
not permit women to accept or gratify their basic need to
grow and fulfill their potentialities as human beings. . . ." [31]

Mrs. Friedan links her thesis to higher education, naming it
as both a major source of the problem and as a possible solution to it. That higher education has assisted in perpetuating
the feminine mystique may be seen in a number of ways,
from the obviously male bias of most college texts on marriage and family, to the notable withdrawal of women from
teaching and administrative positions of colleges. A high
proportion of college women leave school to win a man, or
go to work to put through college a man already won.

Unfortunately, this calculated disinterest in the intellectual
life, so evident in the 1950's, was accompanied by a manifest
disinvolvement in larger issues of the world. This condition,
which not only obtained among co-eds but has carried over
into the life of the adult woman, is reflected, Friedan contends, in the radical shift of content in women's magazines
from articles dealing with world issues, characteristic of the
thirties and forties, to articles focused almost exclusively
upon woman's roles as lover, mother, and homemaker. The
pendulum is now beginning to swing back, but still the great
majority of college women confine their interests to the
sphere of their own personal lives. Friedan believes that even
though the average college woman is not conscious of a direct
relationship between her international disinterest and her
intrapersonal searching, the relationship exists nonetheless.

[31] *Ibid.*, p. 69.

The "privatism" among college youth, at least as it is observable in college women, is seen by Dr. Friedan to be a very direct result of a calculated cultural effort to prevent women from realizing their full identity as human beings. The key to the solution to this problem, according to Friedan, lies with higher education. Her proposal assumes the proportions of an all-out, federally financed program for returning genuinely interested and willing housewives to the university to receive or complete such education as would be adequate to prepare them to assume roles of whole and productive persons in society. Apart from the question of whether her analysis is complete or her solution appropriate, her argument seems undeniable that a major problem of a whole segment of our population may be one of identity—the achievement of selfhood, the discovery of the answer to the question, "Who am I?" Furthermore, she is probably right that higher education plays a decisive role in either the fulfillment or the frustration of this quest, and that to the degree that the campus fails to take into consideration the human identity crisis, it will fail both students in particular and the culture in general.

Betty Friedan's voice is only one of many urgent voices that have sought to call the attention of educators to the personal dimension of their task. Gordon Allport, as both a psychologist and an educator, is zealous in his concern to preserve the ideal of higher education as the principal means of the extension and criticism of culture; yet throughout both his psychological and educational writings, his attention to the importance and uniqueness of the individual student is a dominant theme: "Our colleges are geared to the transmission of culture en masse, whereas the creativity we seek in higher education is the precious and volatile possession of single individuals." [32]

Essential, then, to the university's responsibility is attention to this quest for the meaning of one's self in all the ramifications of the question. The failure of the university to deal

[32] "Uniqueness in Students," *The Goals of Higher Education*, ed. Willis D. Weatherford (Cambridge: Harvard University Press, 1960), p. 61.

adequately with this ontological level and the bearing of this
failure upon other levels is suggested in C. A. Wise's indict-
ment that "in their progress toward self-realization, the students' greatest complaint against the college is that, in the
words of one senior, it has educated them 'for the best of all
possible non-existent worlds.' " [33]

Nor is the problem of identity on the campus a student
problem only. With the diffuse and ever-changing roles of
the faculty member as teacher, researcher, writer, counselor,
and public servant, the question of self-definition can be acute
in him also (though it is framed in a different manner than
on the adolescent level).

Moreover, the university as a whole is suffering an identity
crisis of its own in which it is having to inquire seriously into
the nature of its own being. Clark Kerr uses the same language with which he might speak of American teen-agers
when he says, "American universities have not yet developed
their full identity, their unique theory of purpose and function." [34] Observations like these may bring some clarity to
the plea of students for "a basic redefinition of the very meaning of the university."

So, in the second as in the first aspect of the meaning problem, the issue is both an individual and a collective one. For
its resolution the insights of psychology will be exceedingly
helpful, but not adequate by themselves. Whether the question, "What is the meaning of life?" is raised by the self or
by the university, to settle for this or any one mode of meaning without due consideration of the other modes is to fail to
come to terms with the whole question, and results in the
frustration in which we still flounder in higher education.

MEANING AND THE QUEST FOR PURPOSE

The word "meaning" is often found in conjunction with the
word "purpose." The words are related, though by no means

---

[33] *They Come for the Best of Reasons* (Washington, D.C.: American Council on Education, 1958), p. 32.

[34] *The Uses of the University,* p. 85.

synonymous. The word "purpose" delineates our third level of the meaning question, that which concerns direction and goal. In this sense, the word "meaning" suggests *intention*. When a language teacher points to a word on the blackboard and asks, "What is the meaning of this?" he is asking for definition, our second distinction. Should the same teacher enter the classroom to find a scrawled caricature of himself on the blackboard, he might again inquire, "What is the meaning of this?" In this instance he would be asking not only for the symbolism of the drawing but for intention or purpose. This third aspect evidences itself in such everyday expressions as "I *mean*" (to do something), which is to say, "I intend" to do it.

To ask, "Does life have a meaning?" is to ask, on this level, "Is there an overall encompassing purpose to life?" To speak of a mechanistic universe as being "without meaning" is to say that it is without intention, without previsioned purpose or goal. As Ogden and Richards put it: "If 'meaning' is substituted for the 'intention' or purpose of the will of the universe, then the meaning of anything will be its purpose—as conceived by the speaker qua interpreter of the divine plan. . . . Such a phrase as the Meaning of Life usually implies such a view." [35]

Again, this question does not remain on the abstract, philosophical plane. In the final analysis this level of the question poses a very personal query: "What is the intention of my life? What is its direction, its goal?" It is this aspect of meaning to which students refer who are quoted by psychiatrists everywhere: "I just don't know what I want—I seem to have no direction, no goals."

We speak of this aspect of the meaning problem, therefore, as the *teleological*: that which concerns a *telos* or end, which asks the question, "Where am I going? Toward what am I directed?" Such questions are by no means limited to the intellectually inadequate or psychologically maladjusted students. No less a personage than Robert Maynard Hutchins is reported to have lamented that "I went through high school in

[35] *The Meaning of Meaning*, p. 196.

order to go to college, and through two years of college without knowing why." [36]

One can endure limited purposes, or even purposelessness
for a time, but ultimately the human spirit cries out for something to which to be linked that carries the self beyond self to
that which is more broadly purposeful. The chronological
relationship between the *teleological* and the *ontological*
aspects of the quest for meaning is an issue for considerable
debate. On the one hand it appears that individual focus upon
the more self-oriented goals eclipses larger concerns altogether, that somehow one must make considerable headway
in the personal quest for identity before he is able to attack
larger concerns.[37] On the other hand, it would appear that it
is only as one turns outward to larger concerns that the self is
ultimately discovered in its fullest sense.

It is a temptation, in moving from the *phenomenological*
and *ontological* aspects of the question to the *teleological*, to

---

[36] Quoted in Louise J. Mercier, "What Should Be the Goals of Education
Above the Secondary School Level?" *Goals for American Education: Ninth
Symposium of the Conference on Science, Philosophy and Religion,* ed. Lyman
Bryson, Louis Finkelstein, R. M. Maciver (New York: Harper & Bros.,
1950), pp. 264 and also 271.

[37] For example, the Elizabeth Douvan and Carol Kaye study of "Motivational Factors in College Entrance" (Sanford, ed., *The American College*),
reveals that girls who "hope to gain from college a major transformation
in the self or the self-concept . . . seem to have less personal competence
and less energy for mastering the college environment. . . . They are less
likely to hold part-time jobs or scholarships, and they are less active in
campus affairs. . . . The girl who has a more established sense of self and
hopes only to continue her development in college is more likely to reach
her personal and social goals" (p. 215). Similarly, Sanford maintains that
"it is only when the individual is relatively sure of himself that he can throw
himself into the most challenging and potentially enriching experiences of
life; . . . he must permit himself to be determined by or enveloped in the
demands of the situation or role or task. . . . But this is possible only if
there is an underlying stability in the self-conception" ("Developmental
Status of the Entering Freshman," in Sanford, ed., *The American College,*
pp. 280-81.) Some suggest that because of the necessary priority of settling
certain issues with the self before undertaking to engage in larger academic
or social issues, dropping out of college may not always be a mistake, but,
as Erikson infers, it may be an appropriate kind of "moratorium" on social
growth. (See, *e.g.,* Louis E. Reik, "Drop-out Problem," *The Nation,* May 19,
1962, pp. 442-46.)

draw a distinction in terms of "static" and "dynamic," suggesting that whereas the former two levels deal with "things as they are" or the "self as it is," the latter deals with the "things to be," or the "self to become," or a goal to attain, implying a movement or process. Such distinctions, while tempting, are too facile to be authentic, for a sense of *coherence* must ultimately transcend all spatial and temporal bounds, and the quest for *identity* certainly concerns becoming as well as being. Each aspect of our fourfold construction, if analyzed with philosophical precision, could be seen to entail both static and dynamic dimensions.

Nevertheless there is another sense in which the distinctions are valid. For it is on the *teleological* level, more than on the other two, that the focus shifts to an explicit consideration of the future. It is on this level that the problem of meaning concerns a certain distance—both chronological and axiological—between the reality of the now and the reality of the future. Hence a hypothetical "line" between reality as presently understood and that valued reality previsioned for the future marks one's "direction," and the intention to achieve that future reality becomes one's "purpose."

This is the aspect of human motivation to which Gordon Allport gives the name "propriate striving," [38] and is a mark of crucial distinction from the lower forms of animate life. Whereas lower levels of behavior can be explained largely in terms of drives and impulses directed to the reduction of tension, there are aspects of human behavior which are not amenable to such explanations. They become understandable only in the light of the fundamental human desire for self-extension into the future in terms of purposeful achievement and growth, even at the cost of considerable tension. This striving attitude toward the future is an essential ingredient in one's total sense of meaning.

A reference to the place of the attitude toward the future in mental illness may be illuminating at this point. Eugene Minkowski presents a case of a victim of schizophrenic depres-

[38] *Becoming* (New Haven: Yale University Press, 1955), pp. 47-51.

sion who suffered from delusions of persecution, was a slave
to the most gruesome interpretations of everything he saw,
and genuinely believed that he was to be executed in a matter
of hours. Minkowski lived with his patient in his home for
two months during which they looked out on the same empiri-
cal world but drew entirely different conclusions from it. In
explaining the difference between the patient's perception and
his own, Minkowski states:

> What had happened . . . was simply that I, as a normal human
> being, had rapidly drawn from the observed facts my conclu-
> sions about the future. He, on the other hand, had let the same
> facts go by him, totally unable to draw any profit from them
> for relating himself to the same future. . . . Our thinking is
> essentially empirical; we are interested in facts only insofar
> as we can use them as a basis for planning the future. . . . [The
> patient's] reasoning . . . indicated a profound disorder in his
> general attitude toward the future; that time which we normally
> integrate into a progressive whole was here split into isolated
> fragments. . . . In our patient it was this propulsion toward the
> future which seemed to be totally lacking, leading, as a result,
> to his general attitude.[39]

Lack of meaning, on this level, is a loss of a conception of
how the present relates to the future. The result is the end-
less oppression of the monotony of days which lead nowhere.
Minkowski says that his patient "knew that time was passing
and, whimpering, complained that 'one more day was gone.' "
How different is this conception from that of the college student, presumably not psychotic, who complained: "It's a rat
race, a grind, a meaningless ride on a roller coaster. I'm just
counting the days till it's over!" Minkowski says of his
patient, "There was no action or desire which, emanating
from the present, reached out to the future, spanning the dull,
similar days." [40] How different is this from the void out of

[39] "Findings in a Case of Schizophrenic Depression," *Existence: A New
Dimension in Psychiatry and Psychology,* ed. Rollo May, Ernest Angel, and
Henri F. Ellenberger (New York: Basic Books, 1958), pp. 132-33.
[40] *Ibid.*

which the student says, "I just don't know what I want—I seem to have no direction, no goals."

The missing link in both cases is that dimension of the sense of meaning which sustains the confidence that the tasks and actions of the moment somehow relate to some goal—proximate or ultimate—beyond the moment. To be sure, a goal need not be distant to be valuable, but it must lie at some point beyond oneself, and call forth what Minkowski calls "an element of expansion." He explains:

... We go beyond the limits of our own ego and leave a personal imprint on the world about us, creating works which sever themselves from us to live their own lives. This accompanies a specific, positive feeling which we call contentment—that pleasure which accompanies every finished action or firm decision.[41]

In the light of this psychological analysis it is not difficult to understand the despair that seems to be overtaking the current generation of college youth—the so-called "now" generation—which focuses increasingly on the present. Today's impatient youth display a radical decline of interest in the past and a sharply waning hope for the future. Seymour Halleck, director of psychiatry at the University of Wisconsin, speaks of this characteristic in what he calls today's "elite" students, comprised of both hippies and political activists:

The hippy is a student who seeks an existence in which he is committed neither to past values nor future causes. With his focus on the present he is determined to experience everything he can. ... Despairing of any hope for guidance from the past, pessimistic toward the possibility of altering the world in which he will live, he turns to himself. ... As he turns more and more to the present, his behavior becomes more and more impulsive. He demands instant education, instant comfort, instant solutions. Frustrations of these demands sometimes lead to attempts at self-destruction.

[41] *Ibid.*, p. 134.

Dissatisfied, also, is the more politically active student who, though a participant in movements that actually get things done,

> seems discouragingly incapable of sustaining commitment. . . . Activism is worshipped as an end rather than a means. . . . The subtle self-destructiveness and impracticality of the political, coupled with his impulsive behavior and his clinging to the present, eventually lead to self-doubt and confusion. His activism gives him some protection from psychological anguish, but this is temporary protection.[42]

The significance of these observations about hippies and activists is that shrewd political action will have to seek specific objectives beyond the present if it is to be meaningful in a student's life. It must employ well-defined strategies for shaping the future. The contemporary student focus on the present often results in a fundamental rejection of all strategy, with the twofold result that not only does much political action succeed in little but disruption and the generation of hostility, but it adds little to the student's sense of purposefulness. The concerns of these impatient students are too shortsighted to be ultimately satisfying or meaning-ful.

For those who comprise the university—students, faculty, and administrators—the problem, according to this third mode of putting the question, is not only one of achieving a sense of purpose, but of selecting the most significant purposes, the most valuable and permanent goals. For the student this often means a struggle between what may confront him in terms of curricular requirements and a beckoning toward extracurricular political or social action. It may mean a battle between immediate, visible goals and more distant, obscure goals. One student is reported to have said, "I didn't know why I was there. I felt I should go back to tangible things, such as carpentering." With a faculty member the struggle may be of a different nature, such as a tension between his roles as teacher, writer, researcher, counselor, and public

[42] "The Roots of Student Despair," *Think*, March-April 1967, pp. 21-22.

servant. With an administrator, to whom are entrusted the purposes of the university as a whole, the problem assumes frightening proportions. On this level the meaning of the university involves the question, "What is the university *for?*" a question to which the university responds with manifest uncertainty, as surely as it does to the question of its identity. "The universities of the world," says Moberly, share a "peculiar malaise and impotence. They have little inner self confidence, because they lack, and are increasingly aware that they lack, any clear, agreed sense of direction and purpose." [43]

Speaking more specifically to American universities, C. P. Snow has said: "Your colleges and universities are . . . as good as any in the world. . . . They can do all you want them to . . . if you decide what you want them to do. But at present you have not set yourselves a social purpose of which education is a part." [44]

Meaning, here, is a matter of intention, purpose, goal. To fail to distinguish among these facts of the meaning problem leads to the very obscurity with which we struggle in the usage of this word.

MEANING AND THE QUEST FOR RESPONSIBILITY

To speak of the needs for coherence, identity, and purpose by no means exhausts the meanings of meaning which require recognition and attention. The fourth category of meaning which we may derive from the analysis of Ogden and Richards is "the place of anything in a system."

There is sometimes another possible interpretation in which meaning is equated with "significance." Here the notion of purpose is not always implied, and the meaning of anything is said to have been grasped when it has been understood as related to other things or as having its place in some system as a whole.[45]

[43] Moberly, *The Crisis in the University*, p. 21.
[44] "A Quarter Century, Its Great Delusion," Cowles Magazine and Broadcasting Co.; cf. *Look*, December 19, 1961, pp. 116-20.
[45] *The Meaning of Meaning*, p. 196.

This sounds quite similar to our initial consideration of meaning in terms of phenomenological coherence, which included the consideration of not only how "all things in creation and in history fit together," but how one's life fits with other things. This fourth level, however, is distinguished by a more dynamic conception of cause and consequence, effort and result. Here, the meaning of something is that which it illumines with reference to previous events, or intimates with regard to the future. Ogden and Richards' explanation is helpful: "Some people were said to be slow in grasping the 'meaning' of the declaration of war; in other words, they did not easily think of the consequences of all kinds which were causally linked with that event. Similarly we may ask what is the 'meaning' of unemployment." [46]

When we seek, on this level, the meaning of a particular decision or action, we are asking both, "How does it fit?" and, "What will be its consequences?" It is here that such words as "obligation" and "responsibility" apply. This meaning of meaning suggests that meaning somehow entails, on the one hand, the nature of the response of one's life to that which has gone before it, and the consequences of one's life on the other. The question asked on this level is not so much, "How do all things cohere?" or, "Who am I?" or, "Where am I going?" but, "What *ought* I to do?" Life, to be meaningful, must not only be in touch with answers or clues to each of the first three sets of questions, but ultimately it must be *responsible.*

This mode of the problem we shall call the "cathekontological," [47] that quest having to do with the *fitting,* how one's actions and decisions fit with the "else" that surrounds or precedes them, or, as Ogden and Richards phrased it, the place (of our actions and decisions) "in a system." This mode of the meaning problem represents another area of need in both the self and the university—a need which, as in the case of the other three levels, confronts students, faculty, and those

[46] *Ibid.,* p. 197.
[47] The late H. Richard Niebuhr coined this word to denote fittingness or appropriateness.

responsible for defining the nature and role of the university as a whole. With respect to students the need is described in a variety of ways. It may be couched in terms of "obligation" as in Gordon Allport's appraisal: "It seems to me that the college youth of today is having trouble with his philosophy of life. No longer does the culture give him a sense of solemn obligation to accompany his sense of freedom." [48]

Or the key word may be "conviction," as suggested in David Paton's critique of British students: "They regard the possession of compelling convictions not as a privilege or even as a crime, but rather as a luxury." [49]

At any rate, a well-developed sense of responsibility is one of the crying needs among college-age people. Writing on "Education and Politics: The Problem of Responsibility," Professor Charles Hendel has said, "Education for personal responsibility is necessary to the progress, and even the survival, of civilization. . . . Moral responsibility and freedom must have our foremost concern. To focus on anything less than these two is to endanger the foundation of our civilization and our human values.[50]

The issue here is, as the word suggests, a matter of *answerability*—a question of the embracing of certain purposes as a response to or an answer to something larger than self concerns. It is a matter of purposes and goals selected and defined in the light of what has gone before as well as what is sought after for the future—a quality of action and decision which issues from some sense of "calling"—an obligation, conviction, or loyalty.

At a time when much student activity appears to shun responsibility and flaunt "obligation" (for reasons to which we shall return later), this need for the cultivation of a sense of responsibility looms up more and more in higher education's

[48] *"What Is on the Student's Mind?" Proceedings of the 30th Annual Meeting, American College Health Association,* quoted in Dana Farnsworth, *Mental Health in College and University* (Cambridge: Harvard University Press, 1957), p. 82.

[49] *Blind Guides,* quoted in Arnold Nash, *The University in a Changing World* (New York: The Macmillan Co., 1943), p. 5.

[50] Lyman Bryson *et al.,* eds., *Goals for American Education,* pp. 178, 199.

more responsible discussions of its tasks and failures. In an article on "Developing Community Responsibility," which encourages the development of responsible social participation on the part of students, Arthur Morgan relates the importance of responsibility to the larger issue of meaning. He identifies three interacting factors essential in an educational atmosphere to the equipping of students for maximum contributions to society. Two of these are "the factor of caring, of strong craving for meaning and significance and also caring for human fellowship," and "the recognition of students as responsible fellow workers, not as wards, and full acceptance of the spirit and process of democracy." [51] Morgan contends that these interacting factors must be reflected in the lives of teachers and trustees alike.

A craving for meaning, motive, and significance for one's life will generally characterize significant living. If the trustees of an institution have been chosen for other reasons, and do not have that, then only by accident will they secure it in their administrators; if the administrators do not have that quality, only occasionally and by chance will it be present in the teachers; if the teachers have been chosen too much for scholarship and do not have that craving for life purpose, they cannot transmit it to the students; and if the students do not acquire it, they cannot exercise or transmit it in the communities where they will live and work after college.[52]

Applied to the university as a whole, this fourth mode of the meaning question bears upon the university's response to the host of pressures that converge upon it. It is involved in the questions of the allocation of funds, facilities, and time, the provision of intellectual or social services, the stress upon theoretical or practical research. In each instance it is a question of what is the "fitting" or responsible decision or action for the university. This complex problem of responsibility must be understood as a mode of the larger problem

[51] Willis D. Weatherford, ed., *The Goals of Higher Education*, p. 118. Morgan's third factor is "complete freedom of inquiry."
[52] *Ibid.*, p. 114.

of the quest for meaning and cannot be separated from the other three modes. Furthermore, as we may begin to see shortly, it is the critical clue to the recovery of meaning.

THE MODES OF MEANING AND THE RIDDLE OF EDUCATIONAL THEORY

One of the most generally recognized pressing problems confronting the contemporary university is that of hammering out a definitive educational theory. The foregoing analysis of meaning as it relates to higher education may be instructive to an understanding of the forces at work in the historic debate among various philosophers of education in the United States—a debate that has often been called "the great goals battle." The opposing end zones of this playing field (more often a battleground) represent a fundamental polarity between two contrasting doctrines of man which root in the classical and biblical traditions respectively. The former gave rise to the earliest higher learning in America, patterned after Oxford, Cambridge, and the medieval universities. In these schools learning was principally for the elite, who were given a prescribed curriculum built upon the seven liberal arts for the manifest purpose of transmitting rather than transforming culture. Here learning was admittedly induced with the intention of providing "the discipline and the furniture of the mind; expanding its powers and storing it with knowledge" (as it was expressed in the Yale faculty report of 1828—the first major American effort to articulate the philosophy of classical-liberal education).[53] That this learning was not aimed at any "practical" end was thought to be no cause for apology.

This stress upon "mental discipline" was, among other things, a responsible effort to focus upon the coherence of all truth, and tended well to the component of meaning which I have labeled the "phenomenological." This approach to education is called classical precisely because it derives from the

---

[53] John S. Brubacher and Willis Rudy, eds., *Higher Education in Transition, an American History: 1636-1956* (New York: Harper & Bros., 1958), p. 456, n. 3.

ancient Greek emphasis upon the discernment of order and
coherence, and the obligation of the learned man to see things
"steadily and whole." [54]

Yet when one sits on the sidelines and observes the whole
playing field, he sees that it is possible to have a sense of intellectual coherence and still receive less than a meaningful
education. Reinhold Niebuhr, in an article entitled "The Two
Sources of Western Culture," called attention to the two
kinds of meaning operative in any robust culture, neither of
which is adequate without the other. These might be called
the "coherent" and the "responsible" dimensions of meaning,
both of which our culture has fortunately inherited from its
Hellenic and Hebraic roots.

The meaning of existence is established on the one hand by
the order and coherence of our world. We establish meaning
by any theoretical and practical pursuits which display the
coherence, the causal sequences, and the dependabilities of our
existence and our world. But pure order would destroy the
meaning of human existence insofar as our existence displays
the freedom of the person, his responsibility, his capacity to
transcend the sequences and necessities of nature, to elaborate
a realm of history which is not simply rational because it is
not governed by either metaphysical or natural necessity but
contains configurations in which freedom and necessity are
variously compounded.[55]

"Meaning" and "responsibility" are both emotionally
charged words, the former carrying a positive charge and the
latter a negative one. It is not by accident but by design that
the titles of so many books, articles, and lectures include the

[54] There are, of course, differences to be found between the classical education of the Academy and the Lyceum and the liberal education of eighteenth
and nineteenth-century America. The wholeness of view, for example, decayed
into an increasingly rigid departmentalism. The identification intended here
is that of the emphasis on the value of knowledge for its own sake, that
which glorified the life of the mind as the good life and at least *sought* the
oneness of truth.

[55] *The Christian Idea of Education,* ed. Edmund Fuller (New Haven:
Yale University Press, 1957), p. 237.

word "meaning" and references to the "search for meaning." The substitution of the word "responsibility" would quickly diminish lecture crowds and reading public alike, for the human fact remains that "meaning" is something we want to find, while "responsibility" is something we would often prefer to escape. It is for this reason that all manner of futile efforts are made to find meaning apart from responsibility. Among these efforts are drives for power, easy sex, and quick money which characterize so much human endeavor and which are nothing more than misdirected expressions of the fundamental will to meaning. The futility of these efforts lies in the fact that there is no shortcut to meaning, on or off the campus. Its achievement or reception is by way of responsibility only. The self cannot have one without the other. Neither can the university.

3

I think we should support, or if necessary create, a group of men and women whose business it is to think far ahead of their contemporaries, whose business is not to represent their own country, their own class, their own times, men and women who should be excused from many of the pressures and passions of their own day and permitted to imagine a different kind of world, to anticipate problems and propose solutions to them. . . . Needless to say, we have at least in embryo, just such a class. I refer to the university.

—H. S. Commager

THE RESPONSES AND MISRESPONSES OF THE UNIVERSITY

In the editor's note prefacing Karl Jaspers' book, *The Idea of the University*, Karl Deutsch gives Jaspers' reason for writing the book:

> It was the memory of thousands of students who had forsaken the books of Kant for the loudspeakers of Goebbels and the jack boots of the elite guard; the professors who had eagerly believed the nationalistic and racial propaganda, forsaking their standards of critical thinking; and those other professors who, while not believing the doctrines of the Third Reich, yet found it prudent to pretend belief, and not deceived, yet aided the deceivers.[1]

There were exceptions to this pattern of irresponsibility in prewar Germany, of course, perhaps many of which we will

[1] *The Idea of the University*, p. 4.

A POST-ALIENATION EDUCATIONAL THEORY

never hear. There was, for example, Professor Kurt Huber, who taught psychology and philosophy in the university of Munich, and who, with several of his students, published and circulated several issues of an anti-Nazi bulletin before being caught and executed. Among the papers found in his prison cell were notes explaining his position and intent. One of these contained this testimony:

> Everyone who is morally responsible ought to raise his voice with us against the threatening power of naked might over right; of naked depotism over the intentions of moral good. . . . I have done as I had to do according to an inner voice. I take the consequences on myself, after the beautiful words of Johann Gottlieb Fichte:
>
> > And you should so conduct yourself
> > As though on you alone and on your acts
> > The fate of German things depended
> > And the responsibility were yours! [2]

But few there were who stood by this counsel; the most highly regarded universities in the Western world permitted themselves to become instruments of one of the most barbaric political systems in history.

The real value to us of this bitter memory of German history is the illumination it throws on the very similar problem as it existed and still exists in American higher education. It must be noted that contemporaneously with Professor Huber's protestations, Archibald MacLeish was writing in this country about "The Irresponsibles" in an article in which he predicted that historians of the future may well wonder why the scholars and writers of MacLeish's generation in America failed to oppose such forces as those in Germany "while there was still time and place to oppose them with the arms of scholarship and writing." [3] It will seem to future

---

[2] This Huber story is elaborated in a speech by Eugene McCreary entitled "The Lost Dimensions in Higher Education," delivered at the Fourth Annual YM-YW Student-Faculty Conference, March 4, 1960. (Mimeographed.)

[3] *The Nation*, May 18, 1940, p. 618.

historians, he said, "ironical and strange that the great mass of American scholars and American writers made no effort to defend either themselves or the world by which they lived." The ferment which this article occasioned in the way of both ardent accord and adamant refutation[4] underscores the relevance of the issue in America, and the volley of books and articles on the subject which appeared over the ensuing two decades is evidence of the presence of the problem as surely, even if less dramatically, in America as in Germany.

The present day presents a somewhat different picture from the one of which MacLeish was writing. It is a day of teach-ins and campus protests. It is a day of mounting concern among academicians over civil rights and poverty, South Africa and Vietnam, pollution and population. It is a day in which, as Theodore White has written in *Life* magazine, "a brotherhood of scholars has become the most provocative and propelling influence on all American government and politics."[5] But society's response to campus involvement continues to be mixed. Some charge the scholarly community with irresponsibility for failing to speak and write with sufficient vigor against communism; others for failing to provide enough critical assessment of our own society with respect to domestic and international affairs. Some charge the academic community with irresponsibility for delving into an area where it is presumably not their function to speak out or act out at all; others insist that education that is limited to the classroom is no education at all, that the teacher is responsible for more than the mere transmission of facts. Hence the issue of irresponsibility, while it has altered its shape somewhat in recent years, is as much with us today as it was in the days of the Third Reich.

The current concern for irresponsibility on the campus gives rise to three observations. The first is that the university is a community of selves and will be responsible only as the

---

[4] " 'The Irresponsibles': A Comment" by Douglas Bush, in *Science, Philosophy and Religion: A Second Symposium* (New York: Conference on Science, Philosophy and Religion, 1942), pp. 308-35.

[5] *Life,* June 9, 1967, p. 43.

selves which comprise it are responsible—professors, students, administrators, trustees. The failures of the universities of Germany, or of America, are the failures of communities of selves. The purpose, the identity, and the wholeness or integrity of the university derive as certainly from the manner of its responsibleness as do the purpose, the identity, and the integrity of the individual.

A second observation is that the responsibility of the university is in some manner related to a large human and social concern, whether expressed in terms of "German things" or "the world." The responsible university, like the responsible self, appears to be one which does not divorce itself from the world of which it is a part. This may sound trite and obvious, but we have acted as though it were an insight that had never dawned on us.

A third observation, equally obvious yet equally ignored, is that impassioned pleas for the recovery of responsibility, even if associated with the needs of a culture or a society, are less than helpful apart from a careful analysis of the meaning and complexity of responsibility. Even the appeals of a Huber in Germany or a MacLeish in America must be accompanied by a careful understanding of their terms. Fichte could as well have been quoted in support of the Nazi cause if those "German things" for which the individual was called to be responsible were understood in Hitler's terms. And MacLeish's concern for "the defense of scholars themselves and the world in which they lived" might be turned to refer to an entirely different kind of world and a different manner of defense than that which MacLeish had in mind. That the university is open to charges of irresponsibility is clear. But precisely what these charges mean and what is involved in their solution is not as easily discernible. To speak of a university as responsible to society, to things German or to things American, could be not so much to pose a solution as to restate the problem! There are many and often opposing forces to which any university may feel itself to be responsible.

The Myriad Pressures on Higher Education

In 1962, Dr. Robert M. Hutchins stated: "I believe that the purpose of the university is to be a center of independent criticism, but I do not know of any university that fulfills this role at the present time in the United States. I would say, therefore, in my opinion there is not a true university in the United States today." [6] The fact to which this highly respected educator calls attention, that the university is subject to all manner of pressures which combine to shape and to use the university to their own ends and thereby stifle independent criticism, is readily evident to any serious observer of the academic scene, and is an existential fact to any serious participant within it. Hutchins' assertion reminds one of a prediction he made nearly two and a half decades ago which has long since come true and provides further illustration of the problem at hand:

> Anybody who has watched the development of the American university will have no difficulty in predicting that in the next twenty-five years it will greatly expand on the side of natural science, engineering and the applied social sciences, such as business, industrial relations, and public administration. I have the greatest respect for all these subjects. Perhaps this is the direction in which the American universities should move. But I would point out that if they do move in this direction, it is improbable that they will do so because they have considered the end and concluded that what civilization needs is more natural science, engineering and applied social science. If they move in this direction, it is likely they will do so because powerful pressures in society push them. [7]

Note the distinction between "what civilization needs" and the pushing of "powerful pressures in society," there being no necessary connection, though people have come to think of

[6] *A Conversation: The Political Animal* (Santa Barbara, Calif.: Fund for the Republic, Inc., Center for the Study of Democratic Institutions, 1962), p. 18.

[7] "The Administrator," *Journal of Higher Education,* November 1946, p. 404.

them as synonymous. These powerful pressures are not necessarily evil, but since they are as often concealed as they are evident, they are undeniably problematic.

This multiplicity of pressures cannot be understood apart from their historical roots in "the great goals battle" to which reference was made in Chapter II. It is clear that on the whole, our culture has rejected either extreme of the great goals contest. Neither sheer vocational training apart from the cultural heritage, nor that pure scholarly endeavor which provides no practical or social skills (except for the professional scholar) is acceptable in our time. Nevertheless, these who favor learning for its own sake, those who defend the primacy of learning directed to practical ends, and those who lobby for that learning which enhances personal growth, are all present in the contemporary scene and exert their pressures, both from within and without, upon the university.

As the conclusion of a symposium of articles on *Issues in University Education*,[8] Charles Frankel summarizes what he believes to be the three most critical and persistent issues in American higher education today in the light of the symposium:

> The first is the problem of harmonizing the disparate traditions out of which American higher education springs and of domesticating them within a mobile and democratic society. The second is the problem of finding the sort of moral and financial support for American scholarship that will permit it to maintain its freedom and standards. The third is the problem of establishing a sound relationship between a technologically oriented culture and the institutions and ideals of pure science and disinterested inquiry.[9]

Behind these somewhat restrained and academic formulations of the problems lie some earnest and often bitter struggles with regard to the construction and use of facilities, the

---

[8] Charles Frankel, ed. (New York: Harper & Bros., 1959).
[9] "Conclusion: Critical Issues in American Higher Education," *ibid.*, p. 152.

allocation of funds, the structure of curriculum, and the
vesting of administrative authority.

The problem is evident, first, in the growing involvement
of the larger society in the shaping of university policy and
the style of its operation, for example, the increasing influence
of the business community. This trend is reflected in the
selection of college administrators. Decreasing numbers of
these leaders are being taken from the ranks of the clergy
or from the community of scholars who once were the sources
of nearly all college presidents. Harold Stokes has observed
that

> in recent years the factor of educational distinction has declined
> while factors of personality, managerial skills and successful ex-
> perience in business and administration have increased in im-
> portance. This fact reflects the gradual transformation of the
> college president from an intellectual leader to a manager,
> skilled in administration, a broker in personal and public
> relations.[10]

He also notes that the two college offices which have acquired
the greatest importance today and are demanding among
the highest salaries are those of the business manager and the
superintendent of property. Yet important as these officers
are to the functioning of the modern university, they often
present problems.

> The normal instinct of men trained in the management of busi-
> ness and property is to think of their responsibilities in terms of
> income, expenditures, costs, accounting, balanced budgets and
> operating efficiency. To many of them education is excruciatingly
> businesslike, and they feel it their duty "to bring it into line."
> Tensions can run high between the strictly business and aca-
> demic points of view.[11]

There can be little question that today's increasingly large
and complex institutions of higher learning, having to deal

[10] *The American College President* (New York: Harper & Bros., 1958),
p. 15.
[11] *Ibid.,* p. 64.

now with labor unions, federal grants, and intricate tax structures, require skillful business management. But the dangers of the "corporation image" become sinister when students come to be thought of as "products" and the curriculum as an assembly line, when cost-accounting becomes king, at the expense of those scholarly or public enterprises that don't appear to yield the slightest immediate return.[12]

The problem of subtle manipulation expresses itself secondly, in the influence of these outside pressures on curriculum design. A broad variety of urgent personal, societal, and governmental needs engender severe contests for campus personnel and for course offerings. That higher education should in some sense serve the needs of its society there can be no doubt. The thorny problem comes in defining those needs which are most appropriate for higher education, or any given colleges, to meet. It is implied by everyone who has ever made comment about education's importance to democracy, free institutions, Western civilization, or the "American way of life," that higher education is expected to relate in some useful manner to the "nation's service," as Woodrow Wilson put it.

Yet as soon as one ventures the suggestion of service to the nation he opens up a virtually unlimited range of national needs, from creative social thought and urban involvement to "more doctors and nurses," and from a deeper appreciation of our cultural roots to a better trained army; and from greater individual and national maturity to a source of information for the space program. The questions of whether the physics department will lean toward the theoretical or the technological, whether the history department will be expanded at the expense of a full-time counseling service,

[12] An illustration of the pure businessman's approach to higher education is provided by Harry L. Wells's book, *Higher Education Is Serious Business* (New York: Harper & Bros., 1953), particularly chap. xxiii in which he presents "The Proposal" which ostensibly aims at both the problem of an integrating philosophy and of preparation for post-college life, but is framed in terms that are primarily designed to "reduce the cost of education." At the time of writing this book, Wells was "business manager and vice president" of Northwestern University.

whether building funds will apply to a library addition or to a new stadium, or whether the creative energies of the school's best minds will be devoted to community development or to military research—all these questions illustrate the variety of more or less urgent causes that appeal to the university for its services. These causes may become matters of urgent regional or national need, and thus of considerable pressure.

The task before us in this chapter is to show how all these problems and pressures, both ideological and practical, revolve around and are determined by one central (though complex) issue which is the crucial clue to the recovery of a sense of meaning in both personal and academic life. The issue is that of determining priorities among the many natures and objects of responsibility. Whether one is speaking of the self or the university, it means little to speak about responsibility without specifying *for what* (the nature) and *to whom* (the object) one is to be most responsible. The ways in which these questions are answered makes all the difference in what any given university or self becomes.

The Temptations of Pan-Determinism

In view of the myriad tensions and pressures that beset the academic order, it is little wonder that college administrators feel themselves to be no match for the social and political forces that bear upon them, that faculty frequently throw up their hands in defeat under the subtle controls of college regents and trustees, and that students so often express the now famous judgment that "the only way to get any personal attention around here is to bend your IBM card." Little wonder there is academic schizophrenia, a sense of thwarted purpose, and a loss of personal and communal identity, all of which is to say: a loss of meaning.

The temptation of universities and those who comprise them to think of themselves as helpless pawns in the hands of unharmonious social, political, economic, and historical forces which allow them no real freedom of action or response is as insidious as the mechanistic anthropology against which Viktor Frankl protests so vehemently. Retreats into such theories of pan-determinism are tempting for the reason that they provide an escape—escape from responsibility. But they represent what Peter Berger calls "bad faith," for freedom of choice, while always somewhat curtailed, can never be eliminated. Even in Nazi Germany, as an inmate in a concentration camp, or in America, as a professor in a tightly controlled university, an individual or a group always retains the uniquely human capacity to respond. While German universities in general may have failed to make appropriate use of what freedoms were theirs, isolated incidents such as that of Professor Huber and his students (and who knows how many others?) provide dramatic testimony to the fact that one could be deprived of liberty but never of the last measure of freedom, and therefore of responsibility. Although their decisions led to their deaths, they were nonetheless free responses rather than helpless reactions.

In America the limitations are less severe and more subtle. Yet even when the control of a Board of Regents becomes so oppressive that all avenues of communication and negotiation are closed, freedom remains, as has been demonstrated in a variety of ways ever since the Berkeley revolution of 1964-65. An analysis of this kind of response, in terms of the nature and object of the chosen responsibility and in terms of the bearing of that choice on the recovery of meaning, must be pursued later.

Suffice it at this point to say that the university that would educate its students to responsibility must begin with a fearless inventory of its own problems of responsibility, its temptations to escape them by way of theories of determinism, its failure to see that its actions are, in fact, responses, and that its failures to act are decisions.

The university must begin its task by defining the nature and object of the responsibility to which it is called. Yet this is the very point at which the university needs help so desperately. *The university is not so much un-responsive as it is "mis-responsive."* The lack is not so much one of objectives as of some broad and unifying understanding of the nature and object of its responsibility—one which would bring pattern and wholeness to the variety of objectives that not only are, but *must* be present in the total educational enterprise.

The Power Struggle as a Conflict of Responses

Viktor Frankl's thought brings a certain refinement to Professor Hutchins' statement of prediction quoted earlier. Hutchins foretold that American universities would expand in the direction of natural science, engineering, and the applied social sciences "because power pressures in society push them." But to infer that such a trend was unavoidable is to suggest a determinism which Frankl repudiates. While such claims of helplessness are tempting, a more accurate reading of the situation might be that in expanding the curriculum on the side of technological and practical fields, the university has been *responding* to the pressures upon it. Similarly, when the university reshapes its operational procedures on more businesslike specifications, it does so in compliance with the prevailing practices of the business world. Appeals for gifts, grants, and endowments must be accompanied by evidence of sound fiscal policy and certain gestures of cooperation with the objectives of business. To fail in this respect could mean the early demise of an academic enterprise. Hence the adoption of the business image represents not so much a helpless submission to pressures as a *response* to attitudes of the business community which presently make themselves crucial to the comfortable survival of most colleges.

The question of how carefully these responses are thought through may be an entirely different matter. Dr. Hutchins, at least, is doubtful that curricular changes result from a studied consideration of long-term objectives. "Comfortable survival" ought not, perhaps, to be the ultimate criterion that it so frequently is. To this matter we shall return for a more refined consideration in a moment. Let it simply be noted

here that understanding the actions and strategies of the
university as responses, and seeing the conflicts that erupt
among the various philosophies and programs as conflicts
of responses may lead us to an authentic appreciation of the
nature of the power struggle in which higher education finds
itself embroiled.

Educators who argue, for example, for the more practically
oriented courses in the curriculum are responding to the
needs of a culture which demands technologically trained and
business-oriented personnel to man certain fundamental
structures of our society. This is nothing new in our educational history. As early as 1765 significant modifications were
made in the curricula of New England schools to accommodate the Industrial Revolution and the practical needs of
the expanding American frontier. Similarly utilitarian purposes motivated the establishment of agricultural and industrial schools, spurred by the Morrill Act of 1862.

By the same token, those who defend the need for more
psychologically sensitive endeavors on the campus, in classroom and elsewhere, are responding to the obvious needs of a
culture which displays an increasingly poor mental health
record and has yet many lessons to learn and skills to develop
in interpersonal relationships. So the list extends, including
those who plead the cause of the expanded athletic program
in the interest of redeeming a soft and insufficiently competitive generation, those who support heavier technological
studies at lower levels in response to the educational challenges of the Communist nations, and those who defend the
appropriateness of political action groups on campus as edu-
cationally sound existential involvement in current and
crucial social processes. Need we add mention of the ever-
present lobby for the inclusion of theological considerations
in response to what some feel to be a glaring need for an
early and profound spiritual maturity in our land?

Thus curriculum has been defined as "a barometer by
which we may measure the cultural pressures that operate

upon the school." [13] But the figure is misleading. A barometer records by reacting, not by responding. There is a difference. Curricular construction may be just as automatic as this, but such a judgment is oversimple. A university's service to the community, its adoption of the business image, or its curricular modifications are ways of responding. But the response may not be *morally responsible*. Before moral responsibility is determined, consideration must be given to objects of response other than those often conflicting ones which have been mentioned, and a more penetrating view into the nature and structure of responsibility is necessary.

THE ANSWERING SELF AND THE ANSWERING UNIVERSITY

The obvious difficulty in dealing with the complexity of "responsibilities" of a university is the breadth and imprecision of the word "responsibility." Like the word "meaning" it is used with a variety of intentions. By no means all the references in current literature to responsibility or irresponsibility involve ultimate considerations. But the sober declarations of a Jaspers from Germany, a Moberly from Great Britain, a MacLeish from America, and hundreds of more contemporary voices, combine to make a loud witness to the insufficiency of the many unspoken objects of ultimate responsibility which have been accepted without question.

While a wide range of contemporary thinkers have explicated the concept of responsibility, few scholars in our day have given as careful and devoted attention to the subject as the late moral philosopher and theologian H. Richard Niebuhr. His persistent interest in the meaning and nature of responsibility culminated in his posthumously published book, *The Responsible Self.*[14] Niebuhr did not address himself specifically to the problem of responsibility in the university,

---

[13] Richard Hofstadter and C. DeWitt Hardy, *The Development and Scope of Higher Education in the United States* (New York: Columbia University Press, 1952), p. 11.

[14] (New York: Harper & Row, 1963.)

but his insights apply there precisely as they apply to the individual self.

To the undiscerning eye the battle on campus today is simply a battle between the responsible and the irresponsible, the responsible being those seeking to maintain lawful and orderly operation and the irresponsible being those trying to subvert the orderly process with disruptive activity and unreasonable demands. This view of things arises from an understanding of responsibility that links it very closely with obedience to established authority. According to this definition any revolution would be irresponsible, but as history discloses, radical departures from the status quo may well represent actions more responsible than a lockstep march. Hence what may be taking place on at least some campuses is a confrontation, not between responsibility and irresponsibility, but between two quite different notions of responsibility, two opposing ideas concerning how man expresses himself as a moral agent.

H. Richard Niebuhr has said that man has sought to understand himself as a moral agent by means of a succession of "root metaphors." The first of these was the metaphor of *man-the-maker*, according to which man was understood to be an artificer who constructs things according to an idea and for the sake of an end, whether in the building of an ox yoke and a house, or of a good man and a good society. For the reason that man is indeed purposeful and usually acts and thinks toward the achievement of some goal, this metaphor has been a useful and appropriate one and has shed light on a certain aspect of human existence. A second metaphor is the image of *man-the-citizen*, which has understood man to be living and operating under laws. His intellectual as well as his practical and social actions are here defined by rules and structures within which he is required to function. This figure, too, has been useful because it does indeed express an aspect of the reality of personal existence.

Niebuhr further observes that in both the theoretical and practical realms of man's life there have been countless disputes, as well as many efforts at compromise and adjustment, between these two principal metaphors for understanding man as a self-acting moral being. The result has been a kind of stalemate between two helpful but ultimately inadequate images, and there has resulted a need for a new symbol for understanding man. Hence a third metaphor is welcomed: the image of the self as responsible, "the image of man-the-answerer, man engaged in dialogue, man acting in response to action upon him." [15] This is not to suggest that the former images have lost their meaning, but rather to assert that the key to a modern understanding of man is clearly *interaction*, and that the older symbols are more accurately understood in this light.

Contemporary student attitudes, both passive and active, may illustrate their dissatisfaction with the first two metaphors. Evidence is mounting, for example, that recruiters for big business and for technological fields ars encountering a mounting disinterest on the part of students in entering those fields, quite in spite of the lucrative opportunities offered. It might be said that the image of man-the-maker is fast losing its appeal to modern youth, who hold our society's acquisitive values up for questioning.

Similarly, the concept of man living under laws, man-the-citizen, implying a sort of unquestioning obedience to the laws that are, has been widely denounced. Beginning with the issue of regulations concerning racial balance at public lunch counters, advancing to the questioning of practices governing voter registration in the South, hiring practices in the North, participation in unpopular war, and moving finally to the issue of the locus of decision-making on the campus, students have declared their dissatisfaction with the simple image of man-as-citizen, or at least with many of the laws and customs that seem to define that citizenship. What at least some students have suggested by their actions is that both the creative functions and the civil functions of man as man must be re-informed by a fresh sense of how and to what he is answering

[15] *Ibid.*, p. 56.

with his life. They seem to be saying what Niebuhr had earlier deduced: that something beyond the earlier metaphors for man's self-understanding is required, some new enlightenment that focuses not upon what man initiates but upon how he *responds* to what is initiated outside himself. The clear implication here is that a university and a curriculum designed to do no more than train skilled craftsmen of the culture or produce useful citizens of the society are hardly adequate for the rapidly accelerating complexity of this age.

The Structure of Responsibility: Four Components

To set the tumult of the contemporary campus in the context of this latest metaphor of human self-understanding is only the first step toward determining an answer. Now the question becomes, "How does one determine what, in any given situation, is the 'appropriate response'?"

Niebuhr suggests some promising guidelines. He pictures responsibility as a four-part concept. Response, according to his definition, is the culminating action or change which is made only in the light of the other three components, beginning with *interpretation.*

"All action, . . . including what we rather indeterminately call moral action, is response to action upon us. We do not, however, call it the action of a self or moral action unless it is response to *interpreted* action upon us." [16] Herein lies the critical difference between the "moral responsiveness" of which Niebuhr is speaking and the "conditioned response" of which the behavioral psychologist speaks, or the "reflex action" of the unconscious physical organism. The difference between a reaction and a response is that interpretation is involved in the latter while it is absent in the former. The responsible self is a self responding consciously to what it interprets as the meaning of an action upon it. Whether the responding selves are children and parents, labor and management, neighbor and neighbor, nation and nation, or even men responding to nature, they make their responses to *inter-*

[16] *Ibid.,* p. 61.

preted meaning, and these interpretations are not rational
only but emotional and intuitive. The second element in responsibility is *accountability.* This
component entails the anticipatory aspect of responsible ac-
tion, the anticipation of response to our response.

An agent's action is like a statement in a dialogue. Such a
statement not only seeks to meet, as it were, or to fit into, the
previous statement to which it is an answer, but is made in anticipation of reply. It looks forward as well as backward; it
anticipates objections, confirmations, and corrections. It is
made as part of a total conversation that leads forward and is
to have meaning as a whole. . . . So considered, no action taken
as an atomic unit is responsible.[17]

The responsible man is accountable for his actions in terms
of the way his response takes its place in the dialogue of response upon response. His action takes account of the feelings, convictions, problems, needs, and motivations of those
who induce his response and of those who will be affected by
his response. It "anticipates objections, confirmations, and
corrections." [18]

The other component of responsibility is what Niebuhr
calls *social solidarity.* "Our action is responsible, it appears,
when it is response to action upon us in a continuing discourse
or inter-action among beings forming a continuing society." [19]
In regard to this component, a university is morally responsible to the degree to which its channels remain open and
employed in continuous discourse among all the parties involved. What is required here is not that all needs be met,
but that all sources of information be recognized, that channels of discussion be open to all segments of the community,
that the intricate web of interactions in which all selves and
interest groups function be as well understood as possible.
Only then can the most appropriate (which is to say, responsible) decisions be made.

Niebuhr's analysis does not exhaust the meaning or scope

[17] *Ibid.,* p. 64.
[18] *Ibid.*
[19] *Ibid.,* p. 65.

of responsibility, but it gives us some helpful clues. This may have seemed a tedious and philosophical detour on our journey to meaning, and yet it is only in the context of this mutual understanding of responsibility that we can continue our quest.

For example, it is when this quality of responsibility is present in a university that genuine exchange may take place between administrations and dissident students, or between boards of trustees and the supporting public. With the help of this kind of stance toward responsibility, one may perhaps more clearly discern whether the assumption of a government research contract, or the building of a college gym on ghetto property, or the arranging of a student sit-in or the calling of armed police to disperse the sit-in, are responses or reactions, and whether they are appropriate or less than responsible.

An administrative decision to engage police may be, on the one hand, a thoughtful response to thoughtful or unthoughtful efforts to destroy or permanently close a university. On the other hand, such a decision may mark a failure at the point of interpretation. It can indicate a failure to discern the ultimate intention of the protesters or a failure to hear carefully what is being said. Or it can indicate an error of accountability, in that someone was accountable only to his own pride, without reference to the responses which the students would make to the action. A response such as "No damn eighteen-year-olds are going to run this university" is no response at all, but merely a reaction.

On the opposite side of the controversy, student protesters may have made careful efforts to communicate with the power structure only to be met with frustration, and may have thereupon engaged in a radical political action (response) calculated to bring pressure to bear on critical issues and force communication and negotiation. On the other hand, the students may have merely reacted in anger. Their enthusiasm for the present at the expense of attention to the future may signify a fault at the point of social solidarity, for reason of their lack of concern for "continuing society."

Much student action today does seem to be guilty of not taking into account this social solidarity. Seymour Martin Lipset's observations of one group of students is sufficiently accurate: "Little concerned with the immediate consequences of their actions, the new left student movements appear ready to attack all existing structures, including the university, and to use tactics which alienate the majority, in order to make manifest their contempt, their total rejection of the intolerable world created by their elders." [20] Even when some action of radical discontinuity with the status quo is in order, it must be undertaken as an action of interchange and continuing discourse.

Answerable to Whom?

Conceivably, all the factors suggested above might be operative in some degree in a decision of a university, and yet the decision could still be less than fully responsible. Professor Hutchins could be right that expansion of curriculum on the side of technical and practical subjects may not have resulted from the careful conclusion that what civilization needed was "more natural science, engineering and applied social science." Even the decision that a certain action serves a socially desirable end may not make it the appropriate one. Hence, not only the components of responsibility but the *object* of supreme responsibility must be considered in evaluating the degree and direction of a university's (or a person's) responsibility. Response to a demand for advanced accounting courses rather than to a less vocal cultural need for art appreciation classes may reflect a clear understanding of what the immediate society wants, but still not be what the larger culture needs. Response to certain interpretations of national need may overshadow consideration of more subtle worldwide concerns.

This is not to suggest that the responsibleness of a univer-

[20] "American Student Activism" in *Student Politics and Higher Education in the United States,* published by United Ministries in Higher Education, St. Louis, 1965, p. 1.

sity's decision or action at any point should be measured simply in terms of the yield to the broadest possible social unit. A university which strengthens its home economics department is not necessarily less responsible than one which enlarges its political science department, nor is a seminar on Western civilization always a more responsible offering than a shop course in electronics. Scheduling a concert may be quite as responsible an action as instituting a lecture series on the United Nations, and a faculty-student ball game may be, in some instances, a more responsible undertaking than a workshop for welfare workers.

What, then, are the criteria for judging the responsibleness of a university in view of the varied but equally urgent pleas that come to it in behalf of academic excellence, emotional maturity, national interest, and the survival of civilization? Or, as Niebuhr puts the question with reference to the self: "How is it possible to be *one* self in the multiplicity of events and of one's interpretations of them? How does the self as such become responsible instead of remaining a concatenation of responsive systems, fitting their actions now into this, now into that series of events? [21] The relevance of this question for the university needs no further elaboration.

We have seen how Niebuhr's analysis of the structure of responsibility sheds light on what constitutes "appropriate response" in a given situation. But the more ticklish part of the problem still remains. Having applied Niebuhr's analysis of the *nature* of responsibility to the university, let us examine and apply his analysis of the *object* of responsibility.

The question at hand is, "To whom or to what is one (self or university) called to be ultimately responsible?" Niebuhr contributes two key notions to our discussion: the notion of the "triadic form of response" and the idea of the "transcendent third."

In speaking of the triadic form of response, Niebuhr observes that the self engages in a continuous dialogue in which there are at least three partners—the self, the "social

---

[21] *The Responsible Self*, p. 121.

companion," and some "It" which may be an event or a phenomenon of nature or even a "cause." Almost always communication between selves takes place within this triadic context, and response to any "It" always bears some reference to relationships with other selves with whom common language and modes of understanding are shared.

Suppose, for example, that the "It" is some dramatic natural event, an earthquake or an eclipse. One's response to such an event will be shaped in part by his understanding of nature as that understanding is structured and mediated by society by means of the communally employed language and conceptualization. He will respond to it as a scientifically explainable act of nature, or as a capricious act of an angry god, depending, in part, upon the understanding he has inherited from his companions. Or, if his interpretation of the event departs from the customary one, he will nevertheless hope for some sort of verification from others who view the same event.

This triadic structure is illustrated within the university itself when, for example, scholars of a common discipline, or even of different disciplines, investigate and respond to nature "as when a scientist publishes his theory of the origin of species and awaits its verification, correction, and denial by fellow scientists." [22] This triadic structure would also apply to investigation of social and historical phenomena, philosophical speculation, and artistic creation.

Suppose that the "It," the third component in this triadic structure of response, is a "cause" in the sense of a crusade. Here the response, for example a response of loyalty, is made to the cause on the one hand and to the companions who share that cause on the other. Thus the reference of the self's responsibility "always has a double character. On the one hand it is something personal; on the other it contains within itself again a reference to something that transcends it or to which it refers." [23] Hence the notion of the "transcendent third."

[22] *Ibid.*, p. 82.
[23] *Ibid.*, p. 84.

In the case of a national patriot, Niebuhr says, this "third" to whom he is related, besides being related to his co-patriots, is a nation to which the co-patriot also responds. We seek to educate our children not only to be responsible to their fellows, but to be responsible to something beyond them, to their country and its causes, which provide the context in which the actions of their fellows can be interpreted. This "third" (the nation) seems to be only penultimate, as yet another "third" lies beyond. In the self-understanding of the United States, for example, even the nation and its causes are somehow related to some ultimate community beyond itself in which all men are created equal and are related to "the supreme judge of the world."

In this triadic situation of "devotion to a cause," the university, like the self, may meet real difficulties in determining its response. For example, a university which understands itself to be a community of scholars (or at least that segment of the university which does) is devoted to the cause of "disinterested scholarship" (and to the other communities of scholars who share this loyalty). On a different level, scholars within a particular discipline live by a certain loyalty to their own area of professional and scholarly concern and to the others who share that concern. Or, on still another level, a university (or any segment of it) may understand itself to be loyal to the state whose name it bears, or to the nation whose flag it flies, or to the business community whose money it spends, or to the church who gave it birth (and who likes to remind it of its ecclesiastical affiliation).

In each power struggle on the campus there is a conflict of triadic responses in which the university or component thereof manifests the double reference of loyalty to cause and loyalty to that group of "companions" who share that cause. Civil rights, national defense, faculty salaries, academic freedom, and dormitory house rules are but a few of the myriad causes which provide the substance of triadic responses, each expression of which may represent a measure of responsible action.

But how are one's triadic responses to all these various objects of responsibility to be correlated so that there is a consistency or unity of purpose and direction?

Henotheism on Campus

The existential analysis of Viktor Frankl may be used here to reinforce the theological analysis of Niebuhr. Niebuhr says the problem is fundamentally a *religious* one, since it derives from the "belief-ful" nature of the self and its communities. At the heart of all one's conflicting triadic relationships is his trust in and loyalty to objects of *faith*—which is to say, in "gods." Frankl applies the word *noetic,* saying that there is a dimension in the life of a person (or a university) in which faiths are expressed, values are sought and meaning is derived, inferring that the problem of university integration, like the problem of personal integration, must be approached with regard for this distinctly human dimension which he calls "noetic."

No one is suggesting that every limited cause, every academic department, or every theory of education necessarily becomes a god—not, at least, unless such penultimate objects of concern become objects of *ultimate* concern, trust and loyalty. But the pantheon of "campus gods" is vast, and the recourse to all these multiple centers of value (on campus as anywhere else) can only be defined as *polytheism.* But there is another faith far more prevalent on the present-day campus and far more subtle, due to its resemblance to monotheism. It is *henotheism*—that social faith which makes a finite society the object of ultimate trust and loyalty.

Evidences of the university's operating under henotheistic persuasion are visible on every hand. They are present in many proposed solutions to the problem of disunity of knowledge, such as that made by Scott Buchanan, "that we undertake to remold the sorry and disjointed scheme of things in terms of politics, taking as our matrix the American way of intellectual life as it is formulated in the Bill of Rights and other political, scientific, philosophic, and religious documents that helped and are helping to formulate it.[24] Similarly, faith in a finite society is articulated when Mordecai Kaplan proposes that "democracy function as the basis for normative unity in higher education."[25]

While the incidents are numberless of a university's identification of America or "free society" or "that great state of X" as the object of its trust and loyalty, the finite societies of campus henotheism are not always political. A favorite object of supreme devotion is the worthy cause of "disinterested scholarship," in whose exploration the immediate productive or service value of an action is not meant to be a relevant consideration. To members of this often highly responsible community, the popularly encouraged desire for production results gives way to a more basic yearning for the discovery of truth. To this community, refusal to sign a national loyalty oath is not necessarily a matter of blind obstinacy, but is more likely an expression of loyalty, both to the community of scholars and to the pursuit of truth. Surely these are worthy objects of any man's loyalty, but when they become gods who dictate a man's (or a university's) responses above all other considerations, they become objects of henotheistic faith.

Or the finite society may be a scholarly community within the larger academic community whose devotion to the enterprise of historiography becomes more important than the needs and issues in higher education as a whole, or whose identity with the American Association of English Professors stands out more sharply than its identity as faculty members of Potowatami U.

By no means the least of the idols at whose shrine segments of the university worship is science itself, which, like the state or the academic world as a whole, has its creeds, its rites of initiation, its unwavering procedures, and its traditions. Radical loyalty to the ideals of the scientific community may take militant form. The pure scientist may find himself

---

[24] "The Unity of Knowledge," *Goals for American Education,* ed. Lyman Bryson *et al.,* pp. 146-47.
[25] "The Need for Normative Unity in Higher Education," *ibid.,* p. 304.

in inner turmoil if not overt conflict with the government or military representative who requires a certain secrecy of scientific operation which militates against the spirit of open inquiry and free communication which characterizes the true scientific search. Or again, the theoretical scientist is faithfully defensive against the encroachments of sheer technology, a conflict which may find expression on any campus whose science department provides any services to meet the practical needs of the surrounding community.

As Niebuhr takes pains to point out, religious communities are by no means immune to becoming "closed societies." The prideful "inversion of faith" of which Niebuhr speaks is nowhere so indefensible nor so noticeable as in the churches, and it can find expression in various loyalties, from the dogmatism of a denominational pressure group who insist on a certain biblical interpretation, to the separatism of religious groups on a campus. Even religious societies which outwardly appear to be inclusive may, in actuality, be closed in their faith, failing to look beyond their dogmas, their church, or their Bible to that to which they are called to point.

Another group of converts who can assume the form of a closed society is the less formally religious but often just as sacrosanct community of the devotees of humanism and naturalism.

The issue in the rampant fragmentation of the campus is not the mere conflict of interests, for such conflicts are healthy and unavoidable. There must be a conflict of faiths even among those who recognize the importance of many political, academic, and religious causes among their loyalties. The problem lies in the election of one of these causes as the object of supreme devotion. The maze of decisions and actions that comprise the complex human drama on campus are seen to be responses, triadic in structure, but formed and informed by the respective objects of faith that stand behind them. The conflict must be understood as a problem of faith, of centers of value, of sources of meaning in life, all of which vie for priority in people's loyalties, and must be met on that level.

I have avoided the use of a popular and generally useful word in this discussion—*pluralism*. I have been speaking about the "fragmentation" and "disintegration" (both negatively loaded words) of the campus in arguing that the schismatic condition is deplorable and that some remedy is long overdue. Yet any university that is alive and open in its exploration of knowledge, methods, and faith-perspectives of civilization will be exposed to more than one god and will engage in pluralistic commitments. By its very nature the academic community should be characterized by pluralism; indeed it may properly be suspect if it is not.

One may ask whether some of the commitments referred to in our discussion are "wrong" while others are right, or whether only one is the appropriate one. Is the enterprise "wrong" to which the scholar is devoted to the point of risking congressional investigation by authorities of his nation? Is the fierce loyalty of the scientist to the disinterested and unrestrained investigation of the effects of tobacco smoke "ill-advised" in a school which is in part supported by the tobacco industry? Is the nation's concern to capitalize on its centers of research in the interest of either production or defense "improper"? Do the committed socialist, the renowned parapsychologist, the devout Christian have no place in the academic community? Is civil rights an irrelevant concern to, or arch conservatism a bad influence on, the university? One cannot answer such questions "yes." Nor should one want to. Pluralism on the campus is here to stay. Conflicts of interests are healthy and unavoidable. The problem lies in the election of *one* of these causes, worthy though it may be, as the object of supreme devotion.

Generalized selection is not the answer. To ask, "Which is the most important cause?" is rather like the ridiculous question addressed to Frankl's hypothetical chess player: "In a chess game, which is the best move?" Of course, a selection among causes and the assignment of priorities to objectives of those causes has to be made frequently by every institution. But to draw generalizations about normative higher education on the basis of certain selected causes at the expense of others is not responsible action.

There have been tendencies among some educators to say, "Because you are not designed primarily for the cultivation of the mental disciplines I have no need of you," and of others, "Because you are not oriented to the needs of a productive economy I have no need of you," and then to crystallize these prejudices into dogmas assumed to apply to all higher education. But these moves have failed to bring unity or integrity to today's actual or potential "multiversity."

All this is to say that it is not pluralism but *polytheism* which makes for personal and social disintegration. It is the absence of any overarching cause to which all others are related.

Through the lens of Niebuhr's triadic analysis and with the aid of his concept of henotheism, the problem of academic schizophrenia has now been set in a new and proper framework, namely, a theological one. But still we have not arrived at the formula for integration of our plural loyalties. It is this triadic form of response which holds the key to integration, but to turn the key we must follow Niebuhr one more step of the way.

Radical Monotheism and the Transcendent Third

The problem with henotheism is not just that it is a morally inferior kind of faith (from the standpoint of monotheism), but that "none of these values or centers of value exists universally, or can be object of a universal faith. None of them can guarantee meaning to our life in the world save for a time." [26] This fact, which Niebuhr describes as "the tragedy of our religious life," is the tragedy of our academic life as well. Frankl identifies it as the source of our existential frustration.

[26] Niebuhr, "Faith in Gods and in God," *Radical Monotheism and Western Culture: With Supplementary Essays* (New York: Harper & Bros., 1960), p. 120.

Niebuhr suggests an answer to our henotheistic jumble. It comes not as a blueprint for some new superstructure so much as a topographical map of a difficult jungle terrain whose total contour had eluded us. The contour map, with its aerial view, represents the "transcendent third" which lies beyond each proximate third and gives it its proper place in the whole. Beyond each object of loyalty—national security or responsible scholarship, social justice or self-realization, artistic excellence or international peace—lies a "third beyond the third," which fits the whole scene together like a map.

Just as one's response to his country is a response to transcendent reference groups of, for example, the founding fathers who in turn referred beyond themselves, so one's response to the community of science refers to the fathers of science who refer beyond themselves, and to the mysterious natural order which refers beyond itself. Or one's response to a church refers beyond itself to "so great a cloud of witnesses" who refer beyond themselves to Jesus Christ who refers beyond himself. So one may move, and indeed one must move if his response is to be appropriate, until he refers ultimately to the third beyond all thirds, which is to say the God beyond all gods.

This is the style of responding to which Niebuhr gives the name "radical monotheism"—that "faithing" which moves beyond every closed society to "*being* itself," or I prefer to say "the *source* of all being," through whom all beings derive their being and their meaning. It is universal "faith assurance," the counterpart of which is "universal loyalty." Once loyalty to scholarship and to nation, to professional code and to religious orientation, are seen within the framework of universal loyalty to *being* from which all human endeavors derive, a promise of integration appears, a hope for correlation (though perhaps not the slightest lessening) of the pluralism of loyalties on the campus. This radical faith-perspective not only cements the apparent separations among disciplines and policies but erases the false bifurcation between the secular and the holy. It secularizes all things by denying the

sacredness of any particular being, since God is the principle
of *all* being, and this God alone is holy. Paradoxically, it also
sanctifies all things, since every thing, every community,
every intellectual and spiritual and physical endeavor, all
time and space derive their being and their significance from
God.[27]

The response of the university, of any segment of the university, or of any self, is less than responsible to the extent
that its reference is something less than being itself and its
life less than a life of responsibility in universal community.
No longer do we see the university as necessarily choosing
among service to God or service to society or to scholarship
or to the growth of immature students. Nor do we see these
various causes as synonymous or even concentric. Rather,
the responsible university responds to the needs of the
national *within the context* of universal community and in
so doing fulfills ultimate responsibility to both. William Lee
Miller asks: "May one not say that education serves the
nation best when it is not too strictly concerned to be 'in the
nation's service': there must be something beyond the nation
that it serves, or something intrinsically worthwhile without
regard to services rendered, in order even for education to
have the quality that the nation needs." [28] If the immediate
response of a university is to the interpersonal needs of the
campus community rather than to the need for better public
relations with the surrounding neighborhood, the response
may be an expression of ultimate responsibility because of
its ultimate reference to that which is the Source of, and be-
stows value upon, all communities.

The "best move" in a chess game is always that which is
made with respect to a particular situation in a particular
chess game, but with ultimate reference to the guiding principle of chess playing which supersedes even the rule book
or the mere desire to win. Or, to use a figure Niebuhr likes,

---

[27] Niebuhr's extended discussion of this with reference to Rudolf Otto's
Idea of the Holy appears in *Radical Monotheism*, pp. 50-56.

[28] *Education in the Nation's Service*, Woodrow Wilson Foundation (New
York: Frederick A. Praeger, 1960), p. 180.

the automobile driver makes forty decisions a minute which are not so much the result of memorizing the catechism of driving regulations as of the know-how that is existentially appropriated and translated into a series of immediate responses.

The responsible university is that university which makes no response without regard for universal community; which sees none of its enterprises, curricular or extracurricular, none of the pressures to which it is exposed, and none of the causes it espouses, in isolation. It sees them all within the province of "Being Itself"—the source and meaning of all being. Thus it sees its proximate *diversity* existing within an ultimate *unity*, participation in which justifies for the *university* its proper name. The college that sets this as its goal will recover its lost dimension of meaning.

In his book *Beyond Alienation*, Ernest Becker not only underscores the critical need in our time to construct some synthesis. It is, he contends, the absence of such a dimension that has underlain the failure of Nazi, Communist, and Western philosophies alike. "Without a spiritual dimension to give earthly life a higher meaning, without some continued goal of self-transcendence, man is undermined from within as well as without; he becomes an insular, mechanical thing, wired according to the standard program of self-seeking desires . . . without synthesis and self-transcendence, man becomes a truly pitiful thing." [29]

Becker is hardly pleading for a return to church dominated education. On the contrary, the new moral creed for which he pleads is a "secular moral creed," and he looks to the contemporary university to provide it. "There is no doubt about it," he says, "the whole American experience is floundering on this failure, on the failure of the university to become the locus of the New Moral View of the world." [30]

My proposal is that just such a transcendent dimension is realized by attention to the ultimate faith commitment of

[29] *Beyond Alienation,* p. 72.
[30] *Ibid.,* p. 79.

the university; that just such a synthesis is provided by consciously referring to that object of faith beyond all objects of faith, "Being Itself"; that just such a secular moral creed is to be found in ultimate regard for universal community as a final context in which all responses are to be chosen. The principle of *radical monotheism,* then, becomes the guiding principle of academe—not in any narrow doctrinal or provincial sense, but in the sense of commitment to the god beyond all gods, and in ultimate concern for the well-being of universal community.

This principle needs further refinement as we proceed. Suffice it for the moment to say that it is a principle that will be viewed with the greatest suspicion by the academic community, which has long since learned to mistrust "religious" formulas for solutions to its ills (as well it may, since many of the preachments of the past have themselves sprung from mis-responsibility). "We are not responsive to authority that claims transhistoric and ultimate validity," says Warren Bryan Martin.

> Those who hold to divine revelation and the instruments of infallible authority—the Bible or church or whatever—are restrained by the fact that ours is a pluralistic society where, at least to date, the revelations, dogmas, and priorities of those claiming various forms of absolutism have proved contradictory and unworkable.[31]

But there will be other reasons for the hesitation of higher educators to embrace radical monotheism as the decisive principle of integration, the final source of meaning. The underlying reason has to do with the nature of man, whose primary loyalty instinctively focuses on himself, and who trusts in those objects and causes in which his selfhood is consciously or unconsciously invested. Radical monotheism demands the dethronement of self along with all other relative beings, and of all possible competitors for God's sover-

---

[31] *Alternative to Irrelevance* (Nashville: Abingdon Press, 1968), pp. 149-50.

eignty, the self is the last to be deposed. Therefore the selves which comprise the university are not likely to make this giant step unanimously. Radical monotheism not only brings one's proximate concerns and loyalties into a unified perspective, but often requires a radical revision of behavior and attitude, bringing humility where there was once defensiveness and arrogance, and bringing a willingness to cooperate, even to compromise, where there was once unyielding authoritarianism. Because of what it demands, "it is very questionable," Niebuhr avers, ". . . that anyone has ever yearned for radical faith in the One God." [32]

A second reason for the unlikelihood of any eager rush to radical monotheism is that it is not first of all a theory to which one reasons his way and of which one becomes rationally persuaded by objective proofs. It is a faith, an affirmation of that self which is, to begin with, not rational but "belief-ful." Niebuhr continues: "Believing man does not say first, 'I believe in a creative principle,' and then, 'I believe that the principle is gracious, that is, good toward what issues from it.' He rather says, 'I believe in God the Father, Almighty Maker of heaven and earth.' This is a primary statement, a point of departure and not a deduction." [33] The principle of radical monotheism, in other words, as the determinant of the object and nature of ultimate responsibility, and thus the source of life's meaning, is not deduced; it is "revealed." To this truth we shall need to return in the succeeding chapter for clarification.

THE RESPONSIBLE SCHOLAR

Whatever else the university is and to whatever ends it ultimately directs its efforts, it is, at least in some degree, a community of persons engaged in the scholarly enterprise. Technically and superficially it is a community of teachers and students. Ideally and sometimes actually, it is a community where everyone can share in the teaching and every-

[32] *Radical Monotheism and Western Culture*, p. 31.
[33] *Ibid.*, pp. 32-33.

one ought to share in the learning. At all events, the considerations of the responsible university must also be applied in more specific terms to the individual scholars who comprise it—professor and student alike.

Faith and Responsive Reason

All reason takes place in the context of some faith, and some faith is permeated by reason. Faith conditions, that is to say provides the condition for, our reason. Monotheistic faith sets the stage and governs the style of a kind of reason that is forever seeking and expecting to find unity and relatedness, not only in the phenomena of life, but in the life of the community that seeks to explore these phenomena.

Karl Jaspers captures this style of reason well when he says that the total entity of our lives is made up of spirit, human existence, and what he calls "responsive reason" which he describes as "the mind open to the intrinsic meaning of things," the function of which is to keep broadening our horizons.

> Reason opposes isolation; it seeks coherence. To this end reason requires consistent and correlated, not arbitrary or haphazard, thinking, to bring out contradictions, to integrate every isolated thing and thought. Reason makes us see the kind of understanding that comes from personal experience. It breaks all barriers, overrides all inhibitions; reason gives credit where credit is due and in this fashion preserves the essence of whatever it contemplates.[34]

Such an understanding of reason almost approximates a definition of love. And so it should be, for radical monotheism elicits that kind of reason which manifests a reverence for being and love for all existents within being.

The responsible scholar, therefore, is one who reaches out to, rather than cuts himself off from, fellow scholars, both in his own discipline and from radically different ones, whether

---

[34] *The Idea of the University*, p. 29.

they share his rank or not. The problem of communication cannot be entirely overcome, and interdepartmental courses are less than a sufficient remedy for curricular proliferation. But at least the attitude of mutual exclusiveness is discouraged by radically monotheistic loyalty to a universal object of responsibility. It is not impossible, however idealistic, that such broadening of horizons might even eventuate in sufficient amelioration of departmental narcissism as to replace what David Riesman calls "intellectual veto groups" with broader concerns for collective academic growth.

The opposite of this movement may be called, to play on Jaspers' phrase, "misresponsive reason"—that reason whose primary loyalty is to a closed society often even narrower than the finite society of scholars. Misresponsive reason may also be that reason which invests an inappropriate degree of certainty in itself. J. H. Faurot has written on "Truth and Responsibility," [35] warning of the scholar's proneness to overlook the tentativeness of most knowledge and of the broad postulates upon which a good deal of our learning is based. This oversight often tends to broaden the chasms between scholars as well as to mislead students. Faurot calls for "responsible advocacy" in which the limitations and uncertainties of our knowing are frankly acknowledged. He recalls Ethan Brand, the title character in Hawthorne's short story, who sought for the unpardonable sin and found it in his own breast, "the sin of an intellect that triumphed over the sense of brotherhood with men and reverence for God, and sacrificed everything to its own mighty claim." [36] Hardly a more apt articulation could be found of the irresponsibility of much of higher education to that principle of Being Itself with respect to which all existent beings are to be valued.

Scholarship and Social Involvement

The self attempts to escape ultimate responsibility by retreating into the womb of its own closed society and by set-

[35] *Journal of Higher Education,* January 1960, pp. 1-8.
[36] *Ibid.,* p. 35.

tling for proximate and limited responsibility. Thus it hopes
to avoid confrontation with the larger and more threatening
community. Among scholars this is expressed not only in
disciplinary narcissism but in the temptations to withdraw
from the life of the larger community under a pretext of academic responsibility.

This was the nature of the German professors' irresponsibility during the rise of Hitler, according to Robert Ulrich,
who observes that "with few exceptions, the European professors cared too little about the interaction between academic life and its social and political environment. And this,
it seems to me, applied to the German scholar, however great
his merits in other respects." [37] Again, the very same theme
is heard in MacLeish's rebuke of American scholars:

> The irresponsibility of the scholar is the irresponsibility of
> the scientist upon whose laboratory insulation he has patterned
> all his work. The scholar in letters has made himself as indif-
> ferent to values, as careless of significance, as bored with mean-
> ings as the chemist. He is a refugee from consequences, an
> exile from the responsibilities of moral choice. His words of
> praise are the laboratory words—objectivity, detachment, dis-
> passion. . . . In his capacity as scholar he loves the word—but
> only the word which entails no judgments, involves no decisions,
> accomplishes no actions. [38]

Since MacLeish wrote this, "objectivity" has come to be
seen by an increasing number of observers as a fetish of modern scholarship. As Waldo Beach cogently puts it, "If 'objectivity' means that we are required to look at both sides of the
question and then take no side, it becomes simply a rational-
ization for irresponsibility." [39] Such "objectivity" may begin
with a noncommittal classroom presentation, but it eventuates
in a lack of social involvement. Whether in times of national
or international threat or in the less dramatic periods of
subtler human need, this uninvolvement is, in Niebuhr's

[37] Preface to Jaspers, *The Idea of the University,* p. xviii.
[38] "The Irresponsibles," p. 621.
[39] *Conscience on Campus* (New York: Association Press, 1958), p. 64.

analysis, a response to less than universal community. It is merely response to a closed society of cloistered scholarship or to laboratory science. If it is true that the academic community that permits itself to become little more than a "service station" has not grasped the full meaning of its responsibility, the same may be said of the university that assumes a "public be damned" attitude toward the needs and struggles of the world at large.

When scholarship does rise to the challenge of evaluating and participating in the broader community, its commentary may take an unexpected and unappreciated form. A notable instance in our time is the case of Robert Oppenheimer whose experience exemplifies not only the quality of responsibility demanded by the principle of radical monotheism, but the social risks that may be involved for those who dare to live by it. David Riesman comments:

> I have found it sad . . . that in the Oppenheimer hearings his defenders, such as Professor Smythe, apologized for what appeared to be Oppenheimer's lapses in total obedience to security officers rather than trying to show that Oppenheimer's complex and contextual moral code made him a more responsible person than most of his detractors. The transcript revealed Oppenheimer as a man courageous enough to be more concerned with the fate of the planet than with short-run placating of nationalists—he could guard the security of this country in novel settings because he was less than wholly preoccupied with protecting his own.[40]

The responsible scholar is one who not only acknowledges his freedom to respond (within limits), but recognizes the double reference of his responsibility, which extends ultimately to the Third beyond all thirds, to the community beyond all scholars and all nations, to the One in whom all scholars and nations have their being and find their meaning.

Genuinely responsible action, therefore, will often have the appearance of irresponsibility, as in the case of some students

---

[40] *Constraint and Variety in American Education*, p. 103.

who appear irresponsible to their immediate obligations of
class attendance for reason of their student demonstrations,
but who in fact may be manifesting responsibility to a larger
cause—that of the long-range interests of the university or its
culture. Or the university may give the appearance of irresponsibility in its support of "dissensual" as over against
"consensual" knowledge,[41] in apparent defiance of society's
wishes, but may do so in loyalty to society's need and to the
principle of being from which both university and society
derive, the nature of which, as we shall see later, may be the
subject of more consensus than we realize.

The risks in such transcendent response may involve the
loss of a job, police arrest, expulsion from school, or the withdrawal of financial support. Is it any wonder that the peculiar
quality of responsibility that issues from radical monotheism
is not a popular goal? It is far easier to retreat into the notion
of "collective responsibility," safe from the battlegrounds of
history-in-the-making where the self is forced to identify
himself, safe in the sheltered world of theoretical argument
where, in the name of "objective inquiry," all larger responsibility can be avoided. Again MacLeish thrusts home: "It is
not for nothing that the modern scholar invented the Ph.D.
thesis as his principal contribution to literary form. The Ph.D.
thesis is the perfect image of his world. It is work done for the

---

[41] Frank Pinner elaborates on this distinction in his discussion of "The
Crisis of the State Universities" (in Nevitt Sanford, ed., *The American College*, pp. 940-71). He observes that the state university plays to two publics,
the local public and the cosmopolitan audience of the academic world at
large, and that both publics cannot be played to at the same time. The former,
he says, stresses teaching, the latter, research. The former stresses undergraduate training and the latter graduate work. Consensual knowledge is
that which the public approves and with which it is concerned, in contrast to
dissensual knowledge, whose value or procedures may be widely questioned
among the public at large. Pinner's thesis is that the university is called to
give preference to that knowledge which is least likely to be sponsored by any
other institution of society and which is most needed precisely because of the
widespread misapprehension which it foments. Niebuhr's analysis presses this
thesis a point further to say that the responsible university or scholar may
emphasize dissensual knowledge, not simply because the area of thought is not
understood, but because the principle of *inclusive being* demands it.

sake of doing work—perfectly conscientious, perfectly labo-
rious, perfectly irresponsible." [42]

A RECAPITULATION

To summarize briefly the last two chapters: We have said
that the question of the meaning of life is more than one
question, and that to slight any of the four components of
meaning is to fail to deal with it adequately. This is, in fact,
precisely what has caused the failure of some of the most
carefully calculated attempts to meet this problem as it exists
in both the self and the university. Moreover, I have claimed
that of the four components of the meaning quest, the fourth
one, the responsive or cathekontological mode, is the critical
one—that *the key to the entire problem of meaning is responsibility*. This avenue alone can provide a needed perspective
and direction for the related quests for purpose, identity, and
coherence. To take liberties with Huston Smith's book title,
combined with Smith's quotation from Merleau Ponty, we
are *entitled to meaning* only because we are *condemned to
responsibility*.

We then undertook an analysis of the nature and structure
of responsibility, relying most heavily on the provocative
thought of H. Richard Niebuhr—his ideas of the four components of responsibility, the triadic form of response and
the transcendent third, culminating in the principle of radical
monotheism. While we acknowledged that it would be naïve
to hope for an eager adoption of this principle by large segments of the university community, I contend that it may
well be the only remaining avenue toward the recovery of
meaning in the profound and comprehensive sense for which
man and his communities are crying with ever-increasing
volume in these days.

We have arrived, then, at the penultimate conclusion that
the responsible university, like the responsible self, is that
university which makes no response without regard for
universal community, and that the university, like the self,

[42] "The Irresponsibles," p. 622.

that appropriates this truth is the one that will recover its lost dimension of meaning. In stressing, defining, and delineating responsibility as the key to meaning, we have been proposing a theory of education which, employing Niebuhr's coined word, we could call a "cathekontic theory of education" in which the root metaphor for understanding man and his universities is the figure of *man-the-answerer*.

But we are left at this point with some unresolved questions. How, for example, do we translate regard for universal community, in terms of a given situation? In the confounding array of choices that confront any self or any university in its maze of triadic relationships, among all the earnest voices that petition, inquire, and advise, the persistently disturbing question is: "How does one know the fitting response with certainty?" What criteria are there for assuring that when one hears the beat of a different drummer he is not simply hearing the beat of his own selfish heart or perchance a throbbing in his own deranged mind? Also, is meaning objectively discovered or subjectively invented? To these questions we must turn now as we seek to give added content to the cathekontic theory of education, and to progress toward our goal by way of the principle of serendipity, which is the art of finding by looking the other way.

4

The more faithfully you listen to the voice within you the better you will hear what is sounding outside. And only he who listens can speak.

—Dag Hammarskjöld

There are none living in America today who are more lonesome than the responsible. There are people who have made it their primary goal to form a functional overview of mankind and live within and nourish this view. I don't know who said so or even if it has been announced yet, but every man has the duty to develop a philosophy that he would rule the world if he were elected king. In a small way every father does this if he's worth a damn. Unfortunately for most of the children born since World War II, this duty has been sorrowfully neglected, purposively forgotten, ignored.[1]

—Louis W. Cartwright

What God wants is not our guilt, but our responsibility.

—William Sloan Coffin, Jr.

Like the legendary princes of Serendip, we continue to search about frantically for our illusive prize, trying to avoid

[1] "The New Hero," in *To Make a Difference*, ed. Otto Butz (New York: Harper & Row, 1967), p. 27.

SERENDIPITY—THE RECOVERY OF MEANING BY WAY OF RESPONSIBILITY

the only path which leads to it. But inevitably, *meaning, if we are to find it, must be sought by way of responsibility.*

Niebuhr's variations on the theme of *man-the-answerer* are calculated not only to spotlight the essential nature of man as a moral agent, but also to set in proper perspective the other two useful metaphors of *man-the-fashioner* and *man-the-citizen.*

In special need of this new emphasis on man's answerability are those who see the university through the single-lens view of, first of all, man-the-fashioner. These are the adherents to the *vocational* conception of education, which sees the university primarily as a center of purposeful creativity, a developer of mental, social, and manual skills which prepare youth to "fashion a future," to "make a place for themselves," to "build a world," and other such commencement speech clichés. According to this image, the work of a college should be, at each point, to aim at some good, the ultimate aim being the production of "the good man" and "the good society." We do not belittle or deny this legitimate portion of education's true and noble task. Education does have its goals, and in this sense the vocational image is a valid one for understanding the university. But the image leaves unresolved the question of criteria for setting priorities among these goals and selecting means for their achievement. As Niebuhr has clearly indicated, the image of man-the-maker is not so much incorrect as it is incomplete.

There is also the *political* image of education, a view through which the university is seen not only as discerning and transmitting the laws which govern history and nature, but as fitting into and cooperating with the social structure in which the school is set, and preparing its constituents to do the same. Under the sway of this image, the university's nature is seen as that of living under law, both obeying and transmitting the "thou shalts" and the "thou shalt nots" of nature and of human community. As in the case of the first image, this symbol is useful for understanding the university. There is no denying the political nature of our life, both with respect to our citizenship in communal life and to our existence in the natural order, and education is concerned with both. The fact is, however, that laws are discovered, enacted, and revised in various and often conflicting spheres. The political image brings with it the danger of failing to consider the depth of the university's *critical* function—its responsibility to bring laws themselves into judgment. At one time the focus of scrutiny may be the laws of Newtonian physics, or at another, the tenets of National Socialism, or at another, contemporary American systems. The school's critical function often requires the repudiation of some laws on the grounds of some higher law or something higher than law. Furthermore, those who see man in this image are in danger of overlooking those aspects of human existence (and of university existence) which cannot be subsumed under the concept of law at all. The image of man-the-citizen is not, for this reason, in error; it is simply inadequate.

To supplement, rather than to replace, these metaphors of man-the-fashioner and man-the-citizen Niebuhr proposes the cathekontological image, by which we understand both the self and the university in terms of "answerer." Rather than denying the purposeful aspect of the university's existence, this image sets the university in the context of responsibility, where the kind of "fashioning" that it performs becomes a matter of response to something beyond itself. The fashioning is done in the light of both what has gone before and what is anticipated as a consequence, and in awareness of the total social and historical context in which responses must be made. Rather than denying the political aspect of the university's existence, the cathekontological image views all experiences in citizenship as important functions of the university, seen always through the lens of ultimate responsibility. Thus both judgment by the law and judgment of the law, both obedience and challenge, conformity and transformation—all these find their proper places within the larger context of responsibility.

The particular value of the cathekontological image lies in its implications for the appropriation of meaning. Of course the other images are not totally unrelated to meaning, but

these images are only partially helpful, for ultimately, meaning in life is not found by "fashioning it," nor by simply obeying laws. Purposeful tasks have been known to become woe-
fully empty, and laws are often a hairbreadth from nonsense.
Neither by striving nor by yielding alone is ultimate meaning
appropriated, but by "serendipity"—the art of finding by looking the other way—in this case by looking in the direction of
"fitting response."

My thesis does not state simply that with responsibility
comes meaning, or that irresponsibility guarantees meaninglessness. It is never really a question of "Is there meaning?"
in one's life, but rather, "What depth of meaning is there?"
The axiom I am proposing is that *the depth and duration of
meaning vary directly with the magnitude and ultimacy of
the object to which one commits himself.* His sense of meaning is as large as the object of his supreme responsibility.

Meaning is never either completely understood or completely absent. One is always responsible to *something* or
someone. One always has *some* center of value from which
meaning is derived, even if it is nothing more than himself
or his lowest desires. Hence there is always a measure of
meaning, however meager or short-lived. All across the entire hierarchy of human responses, from those elicited by the
reactions which Stimulus-Response psychologists study to
that quality of response reflected in a Socrates in Athens or a
Jesus in Gethsemane, some measure of meaning attends each
response. There is some meaning in both self-giving and self-
preservation, adjustment and revolt, new exposure to life and
suicide (although it might be a negative, nihilistic one).

The will to pleasure and the will to power are levels of response to selected centers of value, and represent frustrated
efforts to find meaning. The pursuit of wine, women, and song
is a level of response as surely as is the striving for wisdom
and academic position, and the derivative sense of meaning
will be of correspondingly different depth and duration. Both
levels, however, are destined to be inadequate and barren of
ultimate meaning if not related to a loftier object of response
than self or its ingrown causes.

The problem of the loss of meaning in education is compounded grossly by deluded efforts which attack the problem at the wrong point, such as at one of the other three levels of the meaning quest. Take, for example, the level of integration. The cries for integrated studies and for the correlation of learning and life have long been heard, but they have become a mighty chorus since World War II. In response to these cries, interdisciplinary courses have been established and general education courses have been synthesized, thus attacking the meaning problem at the level of sheer conceptual integration. But useful and necessary as such efforts are, the results for the achievement of meaning are less than satisfying. Dismayed cries of "What shall we do with all this disintegrated learning?" have often given way to "What shall we do with all this integrated learning?" Moreover, efforts toward disciplinary integration often militate against the need for clear-cut departmental identity (the area of personal acquaintance and authority) which may be part of someone's personal identity crisis. Seeing things steadily and whole involves more than seeing them all at once. It also means seeing them linked to, and evaluated by, that which gives them wholeness despite their diversity.

Just as frequent, and just as futile, are the efforts to attack the meaning problem primarily, if not exclusively, at the personal *ontological* level—the level of the search for identity. Educational theorists who make questions of self-discovery the paramount emphasis of the educative task are among those who make this error. The centrality of the identity question in the consciousness of college youth (at least the average college youth of the fifties and early sixties) has been abundantly clear, and the dangers of this kind of preoccupation are already visible. By the end of the fifties calls were being heard for a moratorium on the concentration on "self questions." Speaking at the annual meeting of the National Student Councils of the YMCA and YWCA in August 1959, Harvey Cox said: "As a student YM and YW, I think we have been smitten by a hasty love affair with depth psychology, with troubles, with symptoms. Think of all the ink spilled over discovering myself, of unmasking and revealing each other's true and undisguised egos. I think we've had about enough of the Who-am-I bit." [2]

Alexander Miller wrote an entire book on the Christian understanding of selfhood, but devoted it to showing that "maturity may be measured by the degree to which we are bored with the self and with the self's problems." [3]

Similarly, on the *teleological* level, the sheer achievement of goals, whether by way of vocationally oriented curricula or by engagement in social causes, without reference to that which makes the goals supremely valuable, is unproductive of ultimate meaning. A program of education which is designed from freshman to senior years to prepare one for a particular vocation is not thereby endowed with maximum meaning. This is the sore on which Moberly poured salt when he said:

> If you want a bomb the chemistry department will teach you how to make it, if you want a cathedral the department of architecture will teach you how to build it, if you want a healthy body the departments of physiology and medicine will teach you how to tend it. But when you ask whether and why you should want bombs or cathedrals or healthy bodies, the university, on this view, must be content to be dumb and impotent. It can give help and guidance in all things subsidiary but not in the attainment of the one thing needful. [4]

Yet neither is the frantic participation in social causes the sure gate to meaning. At a time when a broad selection of respectable causes from the liberal to conservative extremes of the political spectrum were inviting student participation, Columbia students staged an "all-cause" protest rally with marchers brandishing such signs as "Hoover in '64," "Viva Garibaldi," "Curb your dog," and "We shall overrun!" They

---

[2] Tape-recorded and quoted in Herbert O. Mowrer, *The Crisis in Psychiatry and Religion* (New York: D. Van Nostrand Co., 1961), p. 135.

[3] *The Man in the Mirror: Studies in the Christian Understanding of Selfhood* (New York: Doubleday & Co., 1958), p. 20.

[4] *The Crisis in the University*, p. 52.

thus demonstrated a general disenchantment with causes large and small. This was, to be sure, a different population of students from those who were to erupt onto that same campus five years later. But even today, social causes eliciting student participation, from civil rights to the defense of four-letter words, are not big enough ultimately to satisfy. Any lasting sense of meaning in life that attends participation in a given cause accrues from something more than the cause itself. Campus psychiatrist Seymour Halleck reports:

> There appears to be an inverse relationship between feelings of despair and activism. At the time of the Berkeley free speech controversy, admissions to the student psychiatric clinic dropped markedly. I have noted similar trends at the University of Wisconsin. During a massive protest of the draft which resulted in a sit-in, three of my patients cancelled their therapy hours. In each case they remarked that psychotherapy seemed meaningless when there were so many important things to do. Although each patient was exhausted from hours of picketing, each claimed he had never felt better. When the sit-in collapsed, their symptoms quickly returned.[5]

The ultimate inadequacy of any approach to meaning, important and therapeutic though it be, can be attributed to the ultimate inadequacy of the objects to which it is a response.

This theoretical formulation is existentially illustrated in the checkered life of Leo Tolstoy who, in his lifelong struggle for meaning, is starkly representative of many persons, youth and adult, who comprise the academic community. The hope of achieving personal perfection, the desire for the admiration of his fellows, the zeal to develop mankind by means of his contribution to poetry and writing, his effort to secure happiness for his family—all these were efforts to achieve meaning. But noble as some of these causes were, each was oriented around a limited object of responsibility, thus yielding only a transitory sense of meaning until finally, despite both fame

---

[5] "Why Students Protest; A Psychiatrist's View," *Think*, published by IBM, November-December 1967, p. 3.

and fortune, Tolstoy was led to declare that "life was meaningless . . . a foolish and wicked joke." [6]

Niebuhr calls attention to

> the experience of many a parent whose life had seemed worthwhile because it was devoted to the welfare of a child; the death of the child reveals the illusoriness of the faith and for a time it seems that life is really not worth living. It is the experience of our whole time in which men had thought their existence was meaningful because it served the cause of civilization's progress. With that progress halted, with the possibility of the death of culture becoming apparent, faith seems to be destroyed and doubt of life's meaning enters. [7]

This problem is acutely real to the scientist whose research has been directed to purposes he cannot personally condone; or to the professor whose spirit and substance has issued in a manuscript which does not merit publication; or to a student whose college training is preparing him for a job which may be automated in ten years; or to a scholar whose whole life has been devoted to the development of a thesis which may shortly be disproven. The problem of the lost dimension in education (and in life) will be faced squarely only as one acknowledges that none of these objects of responsibility can provide more than passing meaning alone.

Frankl applies what he calls a "Copernican Revolution" to the question of meaning. "The meaning of life . . . is not to be questioned but to be responded to, for we are responsible to life." [8] Though "life" is a vague term here, it is at least true that this response involves more than the ontological thrust of Maslow's "self-actualization," and more than the teleological thrust of Adler's "life task," for Frankl has judged both to be inadequate alone as avenues to meaning. By the same token, Niebuhr affirms that responses that are ulti-

[6] Leo Tolstoy, *My Confession*, chap. ix, quoted in Niebuhr, *Radical Monotheism*, pp. 19-20.

[7] Niebuhr, "Life Is Worth Living," p. 4, *The Intercollegian and Far Horizons*, October 1939, pp. 3, 4, and 32.

[8] Frankl, *The Doctor and the Soul*, p. 134.

mately responsible are those which are made with regard for universal community, not just of persons, but of being.

There are some questions of academic relationships that can be answered intellectually, resulting in a degree of integration. There are certain problems of personal disarrangement which can be met psychologically, resulting in a degree of personal integration. There are particular matters of vocation and mission which can be illumined by practical vocational guidance, resulting in a certain clarity of direction. But deeper dimensions of each of these issues, together comprising the fundamental issue of life's meaning, must be met, if it is to be met squarely, by way of the door marked *ultimate responsibility*. Higher education, even that characterized by progressive efforts at disciplinary integration, blessed with counseling services and psychologically skilled faculty, and imbued with the highest of public purposes, will continue to come up short in the dimension of ultimate meaning so long as it circumvents the issue of ultimate responsibility. Only by means of such a "cathekontic theory of education" will the university be less liable to commit the all-too-common errors of "intellectualization," "psychologization," "vocationalism," or "politicalization."

THE UNIVERSITY'S APPROPRIATE RESPONSE

The precise manner in which a cathekontic theory would take form in the program of a given campus must be determined contextually. The theory itself suggests the uniqueness of each given situation, which always calls for a uniquely fitting response. We can go further, however, in noting some specific implications of the cathekontic theory of education for the university and for the self.

To begin with, this means that any given university must understand itself as a *responding agency* and must be clear in its own collective mind as to what it is to which it is electing to respond. It cannot retreat from this reality in "bad faith" (as Peter Berger would call it) pleading helplessness. If a college elects to be the servant of a church or a state, the federal government or an industry or any other segment of society, let it be honest with itself and with society about this fact and live with the level of meaning that will ensue. Then, as it becomes evident in time that serving the interests of a business or a denomination or some other closed society without subservience to a "transcendent third" has failed to issue in a sufficiently embracing sense of meaningfulness, let this be accepted as the result of conscious decision. However, if the university is to be worthy of the name, it must never settle for serving such limited objects of loyalty. It cannot stop short of service to universal humanity and creation, if it hopes to appropriate a sense of ultimate and universal meaning.

By this same token, the university is called to confront the individual members of its community forcefully and constantly with the metaphor of *man-as-responder,* and the fundamental assertion that the whole purpose of what goes on on a campus, in and out of the classroom, is to enable its constituents to become more capable responders to the needs of universal creation and community, and that whatever fails to contribute to this end directly or indirectly is ultimately meaningless.

The university undertakes this task in a number of ways. Huston Smith, you may recall, put the task quite simply: "Teachers can help with the problem of meaning both by exemplifying its presence in their lives and by seeing that the meaning import of their subject matter is not neglected." [9] Dr. Smith's challenge to teachers could be implemented by applying our four senses of meaning to the classroom. "Meaning import," to a good teacher, means at least these four things:

First, it means the delineation of a subject's *relation to other subjects,* its dependence upon, as well as its contribution to, other fields of endeavor. To be sure, this calls for a certain humility on the part of departmental specialists who are more inclined to stress the independent value of their respective disciplines. For the teacher to "exemplify the

[9] *Condemned to Meaning,* p. 80.

presence of meaning in his own life" would mean, in this sense, to witness to a conviction of the dynamic relationship of his field to other fields, the mutual contribution of these fields, and the fundamental unity of the knowing enterprise.

Second, the meaning import of a given subject has to do with whatever light it may shed on the question of the student's *identity*. His skill and interest in a given field is part of this. A given course can help a student to ascertain that "I am a natural mathematician" or "I will never make a biologist" or "I feel at home in the social sciences." It is important to alert a student to the "identity-import" of a subject, and part of this may involve warning him against making too hasty judgments about his abilities and potential.

A further part of the "identity import" of a subject lies in the questions it raises about man and life with particular bearing on that individual student. This element is more obvious in courses in psychology, religion, and literature, but discernible as well in courses in biology, business administration, and physics. To return to a much earlier figure, there is a good deal of rare mahogany whitewashed on the campus, a good many stained-glass windows set in places where no light shines through them. This is one way to neglect the meaning import of a subject. A teacher must himself know who he is and understand the place of "I am a chemist" and "I am a teacher of teachers" in his total self-understanding. He must, as well, be acutely aware of this identity element in his students' struggles, and recognize their attendant needs.

Third would be the *"purpose* import" of a subject. Involved here is much more than the obvious consideration of vocational preparation. When this becomes the only criterion for evaluating the purpose import of a subject, the result is an inevitable narrowness. There are the scientists who can't see the slightest reason for a botany major to take a course in music appreciation, or a German major to take biology; the professors of whom Smith speaks who "conduct their courses as if they were boot camps for graduate schools"; the citizen who says, "I am a businessman. I don't know anything about

Vietnam. I'll leave that to the experts, and I wish my colleagues would do the same."

The ultimate purpose import of a course lies in what that course discloses about the nature of the total world in which one is to live, the functions, interests, and needs of other people with whom one may be in relationship, and the whole society for which one will have a share of responsibility.

The weakness of our present schooling in responsibility is often precisely at this point: the center of responsibility is located in too small a circle. If this was imprudent before, it is unthinkable, if not impossible, now. One can no longer absorb himself in economics at the exclusion of civil rights. No matter how technically oriented one may be, a truly responsible citizen can no longer disassociate himself from informed concern for world peace. Whether or not departmental barriers are being broken down by the modern university, they are being broken down by history, and the genuinely educated person today is one who lives in awareness of this. Purpose means infinitely more than a job or a service. It means the total intentionality of one's life and of all life. It means one's potential for joining the attack against all those maladies that keep society from its ultimate responses, all those forces that threaten to dehumanize man. It means that the professional English teacher must now do more than teach his students to amass a knowledge of the language and its literature; he must bring his knowledge to bear on problems of human estrangement and despair, of social comment and of interpersonal communication, and he must press his students to do the same. The purpose aspect of the meaning import of a subject inevitably points beyond the subject itself to history and to creation, just as it must point the scholar, teacher, and student beyond the classroom or the campus to the world at large.

Finally, the decisive mode of the meaning import of a subject, though it has been implied in each of the other three and gives new content to the other three, is the subject's contribution to the enlargement of the student's sense of *responsibility*. Any given subject is a potential challenge to a student's ultimate commitment, a challenge to call into question the adequacy of his present objects of responsibility and the appropriateness of his responses to reality. A course in art or music appreciation may deepen a student's understanding of human expression—both his own and others'—and may even help him to cultivate new ways of responding to life and to people who are different from himself. A course acquainting him with a culture radically different from his own may deepen his sense of responsibility for a larger segment of humanity. A course familiarizing him with some fundamental ambiguities of modern post-Einsteinian physics may alter his understanding of reality as a whole, of the knowing process, and of his responsibility as a scholar and citizen.

Responsible education continually broadens the individual's horizons of interest and concern, and sharpens his sense of responsibility, which will have fundamental bearing upon his sense of purpose, his sense of identity, and his sense of coherence. This is what the "meaning import" of a subject suggests to a university—not simply that it must capitalize on the Intelligence Quotient of a student, but that it must cultivate his Responsibility Quotient, for it is his R.Q. score that will most decisively determine his gain on the recovery of the lost dimension.

THE UNIVERSITY IN A WORLD COME OF AGE

This stress upon the primacy of responsibility is made all the more timely by the growing mood of these times, a mood characterized by a decreasing reliance upon either natural progress or supernatural intervention. This mood is not either simply disillusionment with man or disenchantment with God. It is an awareness of man's vast potential, tempered with a keen sense of his limitations. It is a dismissal of the *Deus ex machina,* with a fairly general acknowledgment of man's inadequacy without some relationship to the "things ultimate" which some call "God." It is a mood to which the word "secularization" refers, as Harvey Cox uses it, as "a process of maturing and assuming responsibility"; a process and an era in which "man must now assume the responsibility for his world. He can no longer shove it off on some religious power." [10]

In other words, the times are calling man to assess his place in creation and in history more critically. He must see himself less vainly than in the single metaphor of man-as-fashioner, for man is beginning to realize that neither the present nor the future can be carefully planned or precisely designed. Man must also see himself less passively than he appeared through the single metaphor of man-the-citizen, which saw him required only to learn of and abide by the structures of his given society. The times demand more courage than the latter image implies and more humility than the former one allows. The day cries for a kind of citizenship that challenges as much as it accepts, that tears down and builds up as much as it conserves intact. It cries for a participant kind of fashioning that recognizes a man's relationship to, and cooperation with, the conditions of history, or better, the Reality behind history. A world come of age, in other words, is one in which man neither fashions answers for himself nor waits for them from above; neither designs a comprehensive philosophy nor plans a flawless revolution for bringing about a new age. Nor does he retreat into a sense of fatalism over the seemingly irrational nature of the universe or the hopelessness of his task of perfecting the world. Rather, he assumes for himself responsibility that he once permitted to be assumed for him (by some church or some state or some society, or by "fate") taking upon himself all the risks and uncertainties pertaining thereto. He *responds* with his own informed creativity to what is given, in full knowledge that the wisest of his thoughts and the best of his efforts are bound to fall short of providing conclusive solutions to anything.

Fortunately, this focus on responsibility seems to be the very thing for which students themselves are clamoring in growing numbers. The report of a national conference on "Students, Stress and the College Experience" notes that "in-

[10] *The Secular City* (New York: The Macmillan Co., paperback ed., 1965), pp. 119 and 217.

flexibility, a lack of opportunity to exercise responsibility for themselves, and irrrelevance are the major sources of stress for today's able college students, not sex, drugs or even Vietnam or the bomb. Such things are by no means unimportant, but they are secondary to the quest for an education which opens the door to selfhood and to an understanding of the world of modern man." [11]

Between the lines of this analysis is the strong implication that the quest for selfhood and an understanding of the modern world necessitates, and will come about by means of, increased opportunity to exercise responsibility. Students seem less and less willing to be simply instruments of conformity to existing structures (the *political* image of the student), or to be simply learners of a role or a trade (the *vocational* image of the student). While not often intending to reject these images entirely, today's student seems to want much more to participate in whatever structures surround him and whatever challenges confront his society. He wants to enjoy a significant role in the affairs of the world at large beginning with the world at hand—his university. In the light of his role as "responder" he will then be more willing to learn and execute his roles as citizen and fashioner.

It is at such points as this that the confluence of the problems of the self and the university becomes most evident. Today's politically active student feels strongly that for him at least part of the solution to the problem of his own alienation and feeling of meaninglessness lies in an opportunity to invest something of himself, his ideas and his concern in an enterprise that calls for the best he can give it, namely, the enterprise of which he is a part—the university. It is as if he knew, almost instinctively, that nothing less than this kind of participation would issue in meaning or give promise of meeting his problem of alienation in any serious way. His "demand for meaning" is integrally related to his willingness to be responsible.

For the university to acknowledge this by giving students

[11] (Washington, D.C.: The Council Press of the U.S. National Student Association, 1966), p. 26.

a larger role in discussion and decision-making in regard to campus problems means infinitely more than simply patronizing the young in order to round out their educational experience. It is as surely a matter of capitalizing on a scarcely tapped storehouse of creativity, and keeping on the listening edge of contemporary student thought and feeling. The arrogant adult claim that students lack the maturity to make any substantial contribution to the dilemmas of higher education have by this time been challenged nation-wide by both action and articulation. *The university come of age in a world come of age is one which recognizes that its students are rapidly coming of age.* Any given university and any individual self on campus finds part of its *raison d'être* to lie in clarifying the nature of the other's existence. It is in response to each other and to their mutual Third beyond, that both will find meaning—the long (too long) lost dimension.

MEANING: DISCOVERED OR INVENTED?

Throughout our discussion of meaning so far we have skirted the issue of whether meaning is objectively discerned or subjectively contrived. Is it something given and certain in the nature of things, which may, by appropriate means, be *discovered,* much as one discovers the laws of thermodynamics? Or is it more like a personal response to a Rorschach inkblot, which would be to say that meaning is what you make of it?

Harvey Cox appears to take the latter position when he contends:

> It is characteristic of urban-secular man that he perceives himself as the source of whatever significance the human enterprise holds. His perception is confirmed by modern cultural anthropology and by the sociology of knowledge. Symbol systems, the constellations of meaning by which human life is given value and direction, are seen as projections of a given society. They change when the society changes and in predictable ways. There is nothing timeless or divine about them.[12]

[12] *The Secular City,* p. 72.

Cox concludes that this mode of thinking, rather than robbing God of his divine prerogative of creating and imposing meaning on man. is actually supporting an authentically biblical doctrine of God. He illustrates this by referring to Yahweh's endowing man with the privilege of naming every living creature and reminding us that "for the Hebrew, naming did not mean simply attaching an arbitrary label. It meant conferring on something its meaning and significance." [13] The whole thrust of the creation account in Genesis, Cox insists, is that God shares the creative task with man.

> After He creates man, He enlists him in this creative activity. Thus the world does not come to man already finished and ordered. It comes in part confused and formless and receives its significance from man. Since man names the animals, the meaning they have comes from the fact that they are incorporated into his life. Their significance arises from their being a part of his projects and purposes. . . . God does not simply insert man into a world filled with creatures which are already named, in relationships and meaning patterns already established by decree. Man must fashion them himself. He doesn't simply discover meaning; he originates it.[14]

One may legitimately raise the question as to whether there isn't a considerable distance between assigning names to other than human objects and assigning meaning to life. Can one "name" himself with the same arbitrariness with which he names a giraffe, or determine the name of the game of life as inventively as he identifies the fish of the sea? Is there not a certain givenness to the ultimate meaning of life that is not subject to the whims and prejudices and wishful thoughts of any particular self?

Huston Smith seems to reside also in the subjective camp when he says, "Strictly speaking, we cannot *find* life's meaning; to a considerable degree, at least, we must *construct* it. . . . The problem of life is to make sense—*make*, not find—

[13] *Ibid.*, p. 73.
[14] *Ibid.*, p. 74.

where apart from this making is nonsense." [15] This, Smith points out, is the thesis that Immanuel Kant develops in his delineation of the categories of reason and perception by means of which the mind *constructs* its experience. This would seem to militate against any notion of an objective meaning to life and to the universe which man seeks to discover.

Which way does one turn at this juncture? Is meaning objective or subjective? Is it relative or absolute? Is it deduced or revealed?

The answer is that it is not wholly either. Smith proceeds to a more balanced explanation:

> The meaning that man senses his life to possess is neither forced upon him by facts nor subjectively contrived. It exceeds the facts while taking account of them. It is neither exclusively subjective nor exclusively objective but something of each. It emerges as man answers in continuing dialogue the beckonings that come from a world that envelopes us while transcending us and all that we know. The meaning does not duplicate what already existed. Just as a rocket lights up a night scene, so it brings novelty into an expanse of darkness. But it was prompted. [16]

The key: *Meaning "emerges as man answers."* It is like the meaning that the artist both discerns and creates as he responds to reality with his creativity. It is the meaning that the statesman both discovers and invents as he draws upon his national tradition and applies it to a fresh and induplicable problem, thus responding with political ingenuity. It is the meaning that the scholar both receives and contrives as he sees former axioms topple in the face of new knowledge and responds to a whole new set of questions with the best of his tentative understanding.

This conception of the etiology of meaning avoids the folly of two errors: on the one hand, the error of waiting for meaning to be disclosed, given outright. The student's "demand

[15] *Condemned to Meaning*, pp. 42, 44.
[16] *Ibid.*, pp. 62-63.

for meaning" is out of order if the implication of the demand is that the student expects the university to dispense meaning along with the diploma. He who waits for meaning to be given will wait a long and despairing time. It does not come that way.

On the other hand, neither is meaning to be understood as whatever construction one wishes to provide. To dispense with the problem so easily would be to respond to little more than the surface of one's own thoughts and feelings. Little wonder that Sartre's insistence on the wholly subjective nature of meaning can so easily lead to ultimate despair. Man neither names his own meaning as he names animals, nor receives it packaged and indexed from heaven.

What, then, of the bold statement in the preceding chapter that the source of life's meaning is not deduced so much as it is *revealed?* [17] If we are speaking of the *source* of life's meaning the statement still stands, but it calls for further probing, if we are to reconcile it with the above argument in favor of deduction.

REVELATION ON CAMPUS

The very mention of revelation or "things revealed" inevitably touches a sensitive nerve in academia. Scholarship is largely committed to the reasoning enterprise and usually prefers to think that the phenomenon of revelation belongs elsewhere, perhaps as an item of curious scrutiny in the psychology department. Our earlier quotation from Warren Bryan Martin would seem to express a majority opinion among academicians with respect to revelation on campus: "Those who hold to divine revelation . . . are restrained by the fact that ours is a pluralistic society where . . . the revelations, dogmas, and priorities . . . have proved contradictory and unworkable." [18]

While one can hardly take issue with Martin's critique of absolutism, we cannot dismiss the phenomenon of revelation

[17] Above, p. 95.
[18] *Alternative to Irrelevance,* pp. 149-50; cf. above, p. 94.

as simply as this. A reexamination of the reality to which the
word refers discloses that revelation is as fundamental a fact
of life in the academic community as anywhere else. It warrants a serious revisit, particularly in the light of the preceding discussion of the etiology of meaning.

Once again I am dependent upon the thought of H. Richard
Niebuhr. "When we speak of revelation," he says, "we mean
that something has happened to us in our history which conditions all our thinking and that through this happening we
are enabled to apprehend what we are, what we are suffering
and doing and what our potentialities are." [19] Niebuhr
stresses that this is not a matter of sheer volition. "We do not
mean that we have freely chosen one section of our history
because we found that it made sense of the remainder. We
mean rather that something has happened which compels
our faith . . . ." [20]

Niebuhr's conception of revelation takes it out of the exclusive confines of organized religious tradition and sets it in
the context of any man's or any community's understanding
of self and life. Whether or not one's understanding is informed by the revealed truths of a religious community, one
is nonetheless influenced if not inspired by revelatory experiences in the communities of which he is a part—political,
social, intellectual. Whoever the self and whatever his community, revelation is essential to understanding. This revelation is not primarily a proposition; it is an experienced event
—an event which somehow becomes part of one's inner history, and thereupon elicits loyalty. It is the disclosure of a
cause which calls for devotion. This may be, to the Jew, that
cause which he understands to be expressed in God's call to
Moses and his giving of the law, or, in some Jewish communities, it may also include the proclamations of the prophets.
Or it may be the cause which issues in the patriotic utterances
of the founding fathers and formative documents of one's
nation. It may be the cause which Christians discern in the

[19] *The Meaning of Revelation* (New York: The Macmillan Co., 1941), p.
138.
[20] *Ibid.*, p. 139.

Cross, the cause of faithful love to God and neighbor as given in God's faithful love to man. Or it may be the cause which one has made his own as the result of a breaking-in of new truth in the laboratory or in the agonizing hours of philosophical speculation. But here again, it is not the proposition but the cause behind it which informs one's reason and action.

Revelation, by this understanding, may not always be good. It may sometimes be misleading and evil, as can be seen by its consequences to selves and communities who interpreted Hitler's rise as revelation. Certain social causes which presume a whole race to be endowed with a natural superiority or a natural inferiority—Jews, Negroes, white men, or Communists—have been inspired (or mis-inspired) by revelation of a sort. Niebuhr calls attention to certain forms of insanity in which erroneous ideas (delusions) of grandeur or of persecution misinform. While there are no grounds for making absolute claims concerning any revelation, there are means of its progressive validation by its continuous subjection to the corroboration of others in the community, and by its exposure to the tests of reasoned experience. While certain fundamental hypotheses of faith may not change, other revealed understandings may be refined and corrected by this process.

Such an understanding of revelation as Niebuhr has described not only bridges the chasm between the explicitly religious community (which is generally presumed to rely upon revealed truth) and other communities (which are generally presumed not to), but it bridges also the false bifurcation between revelation and reason, since "such a revelation, rather than being contrary to reason in our life, is the discovery of rational pattern in it. Revelation means the point at which we can begin to think and act as members of an intelligible and intelligent world of persons." [21] Revelation provides the framework which makes the objects of reasoning meaningful, and makes the community of reasoners coherent. It is the disclosed faith in which reasoning takes place and without which reasoning cannot take place at all. "Such reve-

[21] *Ibid.,* p. 94.

lation is no substitute for reason; the illumination it supplies
does not excuse the mind from labor; but it does give to
that mind the impulsion and the first principles it requires if
it is to be able to do its proper work." [22] It is in this respect
that Niebuhr sees the relation between reason and revelation,
rather than in the sense of mutual exclusiveness and/or
natural enmity. The relationship of reason and revelation is
one of "indispensable cooperation."

Revelation, then, is not the possession of the spiritual elite,
a gift reserved for the mystic, or a hobby for those who appreciate that sort of thing. It is a fact of human life and particularly of human academic life.

Max Scheler, a non-theologian, is one of the many who have
asserted that man must believe either in a God or in an idol,
that man is essentially a believing creature.[23] Niebuhr would
press on to say that just as the incurably belief-ful nature of
man demands that a self must have a god in order to live, so
it requires that there be revelatory moments when the identity of this god is known. This knowledge, in turn, reveals
something of the identity of the self and the cause to which
this god calls the self. Thus meaning is bestowed upon life by
all this revelation.

What is true of the self is no less true of the university.
Although the problems encountered by a complex community
are compounded, the university must come to see these problems as integrally related to the fundamental issue of education's lost dimension, with which the university professes to
be concerned:

> For the most part persons and communities do not have a single
> internal history because their faiths are various and the events
> of life cannot be related to one continuing and abiding good.
> They have "too many selves to know the one," too many his-
> tories, too many gods; alongside their published and professed
> history there are suppressed but true stories of inner life con-

[22] *Ibid.,* p. 109.
[23] *On the Eternal in Man,* trans. Bernard Noble (New York: Harper &
Bros., 1960), p. 399. Cf also pp. 268-69.

centrated about gods of whom they are ashamed. Without a single faith there is no real unity of the self or of a community, therefore no unified inner history but only a multiplicity of memories and destinies.[24]

The predicament of the modern university could hardly be better put. It is evident now that this description applies not only to the welter of varied objects of response that characterize and diffuse the university's life, but also to the diversity of revelatory moments by which its many responses are informed. The university is a community of many "faiths" by which individuals reason and act. How, then, can any sense of cohesion be brought to the schizophrenic campus? What role in particular does revelation play in meeting this problem? Looking back still once more to Niebuhr's thought, and fully aware of the differences involved, we may be able to take some clues from his understanding of how revelation brings wholeness to the Christian's existence, and thus may better understand how revelation may illumine meaning for the university.

With reference to the Christian's history, for example, Niebuhr notes that revelation does three things for the Christian. *First*, it makes the past intelligible by bringing pattern to much that may have seemed disconnected and irrelevant. Because of the Christian's revelatory moments, "there is no part of that past that can be ignored or regarded as beyond possibility of redemption from meaninglessness. And it is the ability of revelation to save all the past from senselessness that is one of the marks of its revelatory character." [25]

A college, let us say, whose history includes a transition from a trade school to a modern liberal arts college need not dismiss its traditions as irrelevant or guard them as sacred, but must see them as efforts that have been made to respond appropriately to the needs of a given time to a given segment of society. A college may abandon certain traditions of the past, appreciating them as appropriate in their own time,

[24] H. Richard Niebuhr, *The Meaning of Revelation*, p. 78.
[25] *Ibid.*, pp. 112-13.

while maintaining other traditions that serve to remind it of
its identity as a unique community. Even past reputations of
academic mediocrity or moral laxity or social irresponsibility
which are now being outlived by a new excellence may be
seen as part of the very motivation for that improvement and
thus by no means beyond meaningfulness. An acceptance and
appreciation of the entire past, then, is revelation's first gift
to an individual university, as it is to an individual Christian.

Secondly, revelation forces the Christian to remember
those parts of his past he had chosen to forget, those episodes
and attitudes in which he had erected barriers against others
or against segments of nature or history, and therefore violated universal responsibility, precluding a sense of universal
meaning. The recollection and appropriation of the past in
all its ugly particulars is a continuing process which is essential to the recovery of all-inclusive meaning. Any college's
past is certain to be as checkered as any individual's. There
are times we would like to forget, and yet we dare not, if we
are to be adequate for the unpredictable challenges of the
future. Revelation reminds us of our follies as well as our
triumphs. Scholarly irresponsibility during the rise of Hitler,
academic silence during the days of loyalty oaths and congressional investigations, acquiescence to the panicky overstress
on technological education inspired by Russia's Sputnik, college administrations' often frantic reactions to student protests, students' occasional overenthusiasm for relatively
minor causes—all these may go down in history as manifesta-
tions of irresponsibility that understandably issued in low
levels of meaning. Revelation forces our recollection of them
in order that the *faux pas* of the past may prepare us for some
of the possible snares of the future and inform our responses
to the present.

Finally, revelation helps the Christian to appropriate the
past of other communities as well. "Through Christ we become immigrants into the empire of God which extends over
all the world and learn to remember the history of that
empire, that is of men in all times and places, as our his-

tory." [26] Revelation illumines universal responsibility, and response to revelation accordingly yields universal meaning in all its modes.

> The apprehension and interpretation of our living past through the revelatory moment may be likened to the psychiatrist's method of seeking to induce a total recall on the part of a patient or of bringing into the light of day what had been a source of anguish while it remained suppressed. To remember all that is in our past and so in our present is to achieve unity of self. To remember the human past as our own past is to achieve community with mankind.[27]

Thus "revelation proves itself to be revelation of reality not only by its intrinsic verity but also by its ability to guide men to many other truths." [28]

Whence comes this revelation to a given university community? What are these revelatory moments? They are not propositions, remember. They are events, happenings in which "we are enabled to apprehend what we are, what we are suffering and doing and what our potentialities are." Several illustrations come to mind. The happening may be the untimely death of a beloved student, faculty member, or administrator whose life gave a supreme witness to what the style and purpose of the college essentially is, or ought to be. Or it may be a social catastrophe calling for a courageous moral response on the part of the college. Or the dismissal of a favorite teacher or student leader. Or it may be a candid disclosure by some eminently qualified campus visitor enabling the school to see itself as others see it. It may even be a campus-wide experience of corporate worship in chapel, or a particular corporate victory on the athletic field, or a corporate creative expression in a significant musical or dramatic production, or an episode of creative involvement in some pressing need of the surrounding community. Any of these, or all of them, may call fresh and perhaps dramatic

[26] *Ibid.*, p. 116.
[27] *Ibid.*, p. 117.
[28] *Ibid.*, p. 139.

attention to the history and purpose and potential of the
school.

Disclosed in moments or experiences of revelation are
indications of the nature and expectations of the object of the
school's response. It is in the course of the interaction of these
disclosures and their responses that meaning is appropriated.

In the light of this necessary interaction or rhythm of revelation and response, it is easier to understand how meaning
may be spoken of as both disclosed and created, or both subjective and objective, or both relative and absolute. Neither
revelation alone, unaccompanied by response, nor response
unenlightened by revelation (which would mean response to
something less than revelation) is sufficient for the appropriation of meaning. In the same sense that reason (a form of
response) and revelation need each other, so revelation and
all human responsiveness need each other if life is to yield
maximum meaning.

Thus revelation represents the objective pole of meaning;
response represents the subjective pole. Revelation discloses Ultimate Meaning (or the gods beyond which is the
God of Ultimate Meaning) while response is relative to and
determined by one's limited and immediate *interpretation* of
that meaning. Revelation represents the givenness of meaning while response expresses man's creative freedom with
respect to making the meaning his own.

COMMITMENT AND THE UNFOLDING OF MEANING ON CAMPUS

It is time to restate my thesis in more precise fashion. We
see now that in speaking of responsibility as the major thor-
oughfare to meaning, we mean that *meaning is appropriated
in the interaction between response and the revealed object
of faith to which the response is made.* Now a further point
of refinement is in order, lest it be inferred that all responses
to revelation issue in meaning. Whether they result from
forgetting, ignoring, denying, or insincere acknowledgment,
there are responses that clearly do not issue in meaning.

Revelation, as Niebuhr has said, is neither a forced event

nor an invented proposition; it is an occurrence which one does not himself bring about but may choose to incorporate into his history. While revelation itself is understood to be a *given*, the self's response to revelation, or the university's, is in no sense predetermined. To claim that, would be to be guilty of that "pandeterminism," that "bad faith" that represents the most sinister kind of irresponsibility. To be sure, one's freedom is limited and one's responses are socially affected, but revelation provides a new opening in the clouds, a new opportunity for insight, a new reason for faith, which one may either take or leave, welcome or ignore. Man and his university are relatively free to respond at any moment in either manner.

A word which has traditionally been used to denote a positive response is *commitment*. While the word may formerly have been understood in absolute terms (one either was committed or he was not), the vast array of recent studies on the subject has set the term in a clearly relative mode. Commitments are known to exist in varying degrees of depth with reference to a broad range of more or less ultimate or proximate causes and objects of loyalty. Each life is characterized by a web of interacting, often conflicting commitments.

Nevertheless, the word is helpful in locating and identifying the conceptions and expressions of responsibility that characterize the campus. Moreover, it comes closest to describing that quality of response to revelation that is essential to the advent of meaning. Our thesis can be framed in fresh words here by saying that ultimate *meaning is derived in the interaction of revelation with those responses to it which are characterized by commitment*. Just as the reception of revelation is more than intellectual, so the response to it must be more than a matter of mental acquiescence. Frankl sets this forth clearly: "The ultimate meaning of man's life is not a matter of his intellectual cognition but rather the matter of his existential commitment." [29]

[29] "Psychiatry and Man's Quest for Meaning," *Psychotherapy and Existentialism* (New York: Washington Square Press, 1967), p. 84.

It is for reason of the necessity of commitment to the discovery of meaning that Frankl has devised his particular therapeutic approach. "Existential analysis and logotherapy aim at bringing the patient to the point of highest possible concentration and dedication." [30] This is a goal not inappropriate for higher learning. It is also an acknowledged objective of high religion. The goal is important not only because the culture may call for it, or because the academic enterprise may require it, but because the human quest for meaning demands it.

It should be expected that each self would make and seek to keep commitments to an assortment of relative causes and objects. But among this tangled web of commitments there is one which supersedes all others. This commitment, whether to family, self, nation, or God as conceived by way of some religious tradition, is one's "religious" or ultimate commitment, in the light of which all other commitments take their respective places. While a measure of meaning is to be derived from each level and reference of commitment, the depth of one's *ultimate sense of meaning* in life depends upon the adequacy and quality of the object of his *ultimate commitment*. While not reducible to a formula, my contention is that the more one's ultimate commitment tends toward universal community and toward the Source of all community and all creation, the more abiding, encompassing, and integrated will be his sense of meaning. Conversely, the more limited one's object of ultimate commitment, the more truncated, insecure, and short-lived will be his sense of meaning. Since it is not simply *any* meaning but *ultimate* meaning, not just transient meaning but enduring meaning which we and the university seem to be seeking, we must concern ourselves not simply with the various proximate commitments that attract selves and universities, but with the ultimate commitments that may capture them.

Kenneth Keniston has written of *The Uncommitted* in this generation of college youth—those who have adopted non-

[30] *The Doctor and the Soul,* p. 63.

commitment as a way of life. Their choice derives, he contends, from a profound sense of alienation which, "once seen as imposed *on* men by an unjust economic system, is increasingly chosen *by* men as their basic stance toward society." [31] Keniston is not referring merely to the alienation between man and the fruits of his labor of which Marx spoke, but to a more far-reaching alienation from and repudiation of current American life generally. Central to this attitude, Keniston says, "is a deep and pervasive mistrust of any and all commitments, be they to other people, to groups, to American culture, or even to the self." [32]

> On every level . . . the alienated refuse conventional commitments, seeing them as unprofitable, dangerous, futile, or merely uncertain and unpredictable. Not only do they repudiate those institutions they see as characteristic of our society, but the belief in goodness of human nature, the usefulness of group activities, and the possibility or utility of political and civic activities, closeness and intimacy with others, or even a resolute commitment to action or responsibility. The rejection of American society is but one part of a more global distrust of any commitment. [33]

Alienated youth think of any commitment as giving up their freedom and autonomy. They yearn for total freedom, believing that the least restriction would represent a sacrifice of individuality, a compromise of their integrity. Therefore they shun the very responsibility without which there is, in truth, no freedom but only self-indulgence and, even more tragic, no meaning.

In the light of the thesis I am proposing, it is little wonder that so many of the alienated find life in general and college life in particular meaningless and irrelevant. Just as ultimate meaning will be the fruit only of ultimate commitment, so the predictable result of a *lack* of commitment and evasion of responsibility is no meaning at all.

[31] *The Uncommitted* (New York: Harcourt, Brace & World, 1965), p. 3.
[32] *Ibid.*, p. 56.
[33] *Ibid.*, p. 60.

It is important that the causal relation here not be misinterpreted lest efforts be made to attack the problem at the wrong end. People are not uncommitted because there is no meaning; there is no meaning because they are uncommitted, or insufficiently committed, or inappropriately committed. The issue of commitment falls at the inceptive rather than at the derivative end of the meaning quest. In arguing this point one becomes aware of the artificiality of attaching temporal sequences to a problem so latticed with mutual dependencies and interrelationships. Yet the point is crucial, for efforts to deal with meaning apart from commitment are legion, and the hopes for deriving ultimate meaning from proximate commitments are as universal as they are doomed to ultimate frustration.

There may be a temptation to reverse the direction of this thesis by observing that one makes commitments only to things, objects or causes that are in some sense already meaningful. To be sure, commitments are made only to that which at least gives promise of ultimate meaning. But this level of meaning's discernment is largely intellectual and is not genuinely appropriated, except by the personal act of commitment and trust.

We shall look briefly at two particular arenas of university experience in which we may find illustrations of this thesis that meaning unfolds from those responses to revelation characterized by commitment. The first of these is the arena of *scholarly pursuit* itself. The ideal of academic "objectivity," assessed by many today as an ultimately impossible goal, has been criticized by many others as at least irresponsible in its intent. When one fails or refuses to commit himself and to profess a single academically responsible viewpoint, this can be an expression of irresponsibility. One who comes to no conclusions repudiates the relevance of his scholarship to the good or ill of the world, or, acknowledging its relevance, fails to lend the weight of his life and thought in the direction of his conclusions. Thus he may, indeed, be guilty of irresponsibility.

Of course there is another sense in which "objectivity"

does not represent irresponsibility at all, in which commitment to a single point of view may, in fact, be the irresponsible alternative. The clue lies in the placement of ultimate commitment. Nearly every academician has encountered (and no doubt has himself manifested at times) such a depth of commitment to a particular perspective or school of thought that it has become a veritable part of the core of his being. At such times, threats to the stability of his ideological position become virtual threats to the scholar's own existence. Academic debates are almost never sheerly intellectual. They customarily involve the whole being of strongly committed scholars, and the deeper the commitment to the theses espoused, the more existentially involved the debaters become in the fate of their theses. Likewise, the more radical their commitment to this thesis becomes, the more their sense of meaning (in terms of the purposefulness of their labor, their identity as scholars, and their view of total reality, as perceived both intellectually and existentially) rises or falls with the thesis.

Although such commitment may contribute to the total academic exploration by its persuasive illumination of one fact of truth, an obvious danger lies in its attaining a status of ultimacy. The consequence of this misplacement is that the discernment of truth becomes less important than the defense of the thesis, and the larger objectives of unbiased honesty become overshadowed by the narrow objectives of a limited perspective within a given speciality of a certain school of thought. By making ultimate a commitment which should be proximate, the academician not only impedes the scholarly enterprise by fending off new disclosures and closing his mind to the possibility of revised understandings, but he destines himself to derive modes of meaning commensurate with the tentative and limited object of his intellectual efforts. While scholarly "objectivity" may become irresponsible, its intent is to encourage enough detachment so that the kind of overzealous personal involvement which impedes the search for truth may be avoided.

The ideal is not necessarily either of these alternatives.

Neither the commitment to a certain perspective, nor the effort toward personal detachment from limited perspectives is to be sought exclusively, but neither is it to be avoided, as if it in itself were a sin. The deciding factor is the appropriateness of response to proximate, as over against ultimate, objects of loyalty. It must simply be kept in mind that beyond the commitment to any point of view is one's commitment to the discovery of truth, for the sake of which the point of view is pursued, presumably. Beyond this commitment may lie a still higher allegiance—to the Source of all truth, to Being Itself (which some of us call "God"), whose truth is in the process of being discerned, bit by bit, and for whose sake the whole knowing enterprise is undertaken. The sense of meaning that unfolds from commitment to a "cause" of these proportions outlasts the shifting ideological tides.

In *responding* with ultimate commitment to Being Itself, one's *purpose* becomes one of thinking God's thoughts after him and recognizing the continuing need for the revision of one's relative and incomplete formulations. One's *identity* becomes that of a scholar in search of truth in companionship with others of radically different persuasions, whose proximate tasks and immediate convictions differ greatly but whose ultimate commitment is attached to nothing less than universal community, universal truth, Being Itself. The sense of *integration* which results is not threatened either by radical difference of opinion or diversity of activity. This genuinely responsible kind of commitment permits both paradox and uncertainty because ultimate trust has not been placed in either the popularity of certain ideas nor in the capacities of the human intellect. When ultimate commitment is placed in that which transcends all scholarly endeavor, then axioms proven wrong are seen to be as valuable to the total enterprise as axioms proven right, and meaning abides in spite of, perhaps even because of, radical transformations in long-held theologies. And from commitment to the ultimate arises ultimate meaning.

A second arena in which our thesis may be tested is that of *involvement in social issues,* a subject which has not lacked for publicity in recent years. For some time a variety of social causes which have been open to college youth were largely ignored, but an increasing minority of students are now responding to the call of VISTA, the Peace Corps, and other agencies of human service. They are not only participating in demonstrations and campaigning for political candidates, but demanding participation in the restructuring of higher education itself. The full range of social and historical factors which would explain this changing picture has yet to be researched, but it does seem evident that the comparative popularity of the various social causes in which college youth are participating reflects the comparative importance of the *reference of response* to which the cause addresses itself. A demonstration in behalf of four-letter words, for instance, since it devotes itself to the personal tastes of a few people, draws little sustained interest. The cause of racial justice, on the other hand, has commanded almost universal response on the campus, much of which response has exhibited prolonged, sacrificial loyalty. It is my contention that the major reason for the difference in student response has depended primarily on the difference in magnitude of the *objects* of the responses. Obviously, impassioned leadership makes a difference, as do such other factors as the time of year, the openness or oppressiveness of the existing systems, the political climate of the community (both local and national), etc. But when students are confronted with a big enough cause and when there is freedom for leadership (good or bad) to develop, youth will go to any end of sacrifice to make their contribution. The larger the cause, the more avidly they will defend it. Repressive measures on the part of opponents of the objectives which represent the cause only strengthen the resolve of its adherents.

The civil rights cause, since it represents the welfare of a broad segment of human community, elicits all measure of involvement on the part of students. And the consequence of their existential commitment to this cause is a revived sense of "fitting in" or belonging, of identification and integrity as persons, and of noble and valuable purpose in the world (the

first three modes of meaning). An interesting outgrowth of
the civil rights movement has been the reinstatement of
professions of ultimate concern (religious language) as
respectable expression on the campus. A folk singer speaks
of the importance of love as a strategy—a message the Christian church has been trying to preach to students (and to
everybody else) for decades—or in the heat of a mass demonstration a crowd of students and faculty participants sing *The
Lord's Prayer* together. These are indications that the cause
of racial justice is understood (by some students at least) in
the context of a larger object of responsibility than either race
or justice. Needless to add, far more life-meaning results
from this cause than from such causes as the "four-letter
word campaign," or the liberalization of house rules, or even
the defense of a maligned faculty member.

Once again what we are suggesting is that the sense of
meaning which is recovered in its respective modes on the
part of the participants of any movement is directly related
to the transcendency of their cause. Moreover, the participants' existential commitment, however vague their transcendent reference may be, may set in a new perspective many
other issues, such as the proper function of institutions of
higher learning, the purposes of their education, and the
question of their post-college role in society. Indeed, these
results of heightened and broadened concerns have occurred
on our campuses to a degree that has astounded and fright-
ened the adult generation, many of whose largest concern
when they were in college was how to get into the "right"
fraternity.

The question of the university's function as a whole having been raised, let us test our thesis finally on *the university
as an institution*. Recall Clark Kerr's observation that "American universities have not yet developed their full identity,
their unique theory of purpose and function." [34] The implication of my thought is that the ontological and teleological loss
of meaning on the campus will continue until the university

[34] *The Uses of the University*, p. 85.

responds by way of commitment to some object whose cause is transcendent to each proximate cause on campus.

There are some institutions to which Dr. Kerr's comments would not appear to be applicable, of course. In a military academy such as West Point, for instance, whose ultimate commitment is clearly pledged to the armed service of the federal government, there is little question concerning either purpose or identity. With this strict definition of responsibility comes the meaning of the school's existence. (This is not to say that certain individuals within the institution may not be quite unsure of their own ultimate commitments and thus of the ultimate meaning of their school experience.) But the commitments of most schools are more diffuse than those of a military academy, and consequently their function and identity is far less decisive. But I contend that not until such time as a given school approaches the depth of commitment of a military academy (though hopefully to a more universal cause) do we have reason to expect that the institution will be rescued from the state which I call the "Ichabod Crane syndrome"—the tendency to get on the old horse and ride off in all directions at once.

A cathekontological theory of education, then, is one which encourages the self and the university to assist each other to a recovery of meaning by means of a focus on the fitting object and nature of responsiveness. We cannot propose specific blueprints for student action, for revisions of curriculum or for reformation of structure. The very intention of the cathekontic emphasis is to recognize the uniqueness of each given situation, which always calls for a uniquely fitting response. Hence the manner in which these suggestions take form on a given campus must be determined contextually. The response called for in a given context—which is to say on a given campus at a given time—will need to be inventive and ingenious. What must be developed is something more on the order of a style than a program, a stance rather that a strategy. But the key word is *flexibility,* the lack of which is precisely one of the major student complaints of the day.

5

Institutions of higher learning must now move. . . . If models are no longer provided by other social institutions, and if, like it or not, education is the new religion of the young, then we have no honorable alternative but to take up the responsibility of leadership, not only in such areas as social graces, job training, and surface preparation for citizenship, but also in those having to do with philosophy and religion—objectives, values, and standards.

—Warren Bryan Martin[1]

For my part I do not know how to make clear what is at stake other than by simply asserting that the questions which are finally of most importance to all of us in our private lives and for the health of our "selves" are not the questions which secular inquiry normally asks of nature, important as these are. They are rather the questions which religion *answers* for her believers by supplying meaning to life, by kindling hope, and by giving, through faith in God, a basis for ethical behavior.

—Nathan Pusey[2]

I should like to add that [man] is often much more religious than he suspects.

—Viktor Frankl[3]

[1] *Alternative to Irrelevance*, p. 148.

[2] "Secularism and the Joy of Belief," *Age of the Scholar: Observations on Education in a Troubled Decade* (Cambridge: Belknap Press [Harvard University Press], 1963), p. 98.

[3] *The Doctor and the Soul*, p. xx.

THE FAITH OF A SECULAR UNIVERSITY

THE SELF, THE UNIVERSITY, AND THE SEARCH FOR MEANING

The questions which have occupied our attention throughout this study are those which are not only "of most importance to all of us in our private lives," as educator Pusey suggests, but of utmost importance in the life of the university. Values, commitments, identity, purpose, meaning, and responsibility are all words which appear with increasing frequency in discussions of higher education in both popular and professional press. They concern the university not only because they are the problems of the selves who comprise the university, but because they are problems of the university as a community.

These problems, at their deepest levels, are frankly religious problems and cannot be approached except by way of direct confrontation with the fact and necessity of religion. Proximate values and commitments can be shared, selected, and argued without reference to religious considerations. But as soon as one turns to the question of *ultimate* values and commitments, as soon he must if other values and commitments are to assume some perspective, then he has entered the province of *religion*. One can deal with proximate responsibilities on the social and political level, but as soon as one begins to discuss his ultimate responsibility he has begun to expose his religion. There are "meanings" and there are "meanings," but once one gets beyond the limited and dissatisfying "meanings" that comprise his daily existence and dares to pursue the question of "the meaning of it all," he has embarked upon the quest which is, by definition, religious.[4]

The ultimately religious nature of questions of value is asserted by philosopher and mathematician Alfred North Whitehead, who relates religion and responsibility (which he prefers to call "duty") to the educational enterprise.

We can be content with no less than the old summary of educational ideals which has been current at any time from the dawn

---

[4] One Latin root of the word "religious" is *re-ligare*, to tie up or to bind together.

of civilization. The essence of education is that it be religious. . . . A religious education is an education which inculcates duty and reverence. Duty arises from our potential control over events. . . . And the foundation of reverence is this perception, that the present holds within itself the complete scheme of existence.[5]

Bernard Eugene Meland notes that the major tendency in all areas of creative thought today—physics, biology, psychology, contextualism in ethics, and certain kinds of metaphysics —is toward relational thinking, and that this is clearly "a religious tendency in that it provides a perspective for thinking in which religious meanings may be discerned." [6]

The relationships of meaning, value, and responsibility to religion help to expose a fact of paramount importance. *If* educators are in earnest in their almost frantic efforts to revitalize a consideration of values in the academic enterprise, and *if* educators mean what they say when they deplore the irresponsibility of students and often faculty and even educational institutions as a whole, and *if* educators are genuine in their concern to recover a sense of meaning in the complex and fragmented university experience, then there is no way to avoid the conclusion that their invectives are inwardly and actually pleas for the recovery of *religion* in the most fundamental sense of the word. *The lost dimension in education is the religious dimension*—the dimension of meaning and value, of faith and commitment, of relationship with and responsibility to that which is conceived to be *ultimate* in the universe.

The various existential frustrations of the contemporary university are evidences of the folly of trying to dispense with religion while at the same time hoping to enjoy its fruits. One bypasses religion only at the expense of all the questions and some of the answers concerning the ultimate meaning of life. One tries to isolate matters of faith and delegate them to

[5] *The Aims of Education* (New York: The Macmillan Co., 1929 [Mentor Book]), p. 26.

[6] *Higher Education and the Human Spirit* (Chicago: University of Chicago Press, 1953), p. 24.

local churches or to "the religious types" on campus only at great peril to the whole reasoning enterprise. In postponing matters of the *spirit* in education until the day of the Baccalaureate one reduces man to a rational biped with certain somatic interests (or in some instances the other way around). Whereas higher education has been inclined to think of religion as an appendage to the curriculum or as an *activity* of the extracurriculum which church colleges have and state universities do not, religion is rather a *dimension* of the entire human (including academic) enterprise.

This dimensionality becomes evident whenever persons trust, or make commitments, whenever a university defines its actions by loyalty to a center of value or understands itself to be engaged in an enterprise that ultimately has meaning, or bears reference to something more than a social reality. A sectarian doctrine may be optional and a denominational practice only elective, but religion is the most fundamentally required area of human exploration. It is ignored at the cost of personal and national integrity and ultimate coherence.

Despite all this, the attitude of much current higher education (meaning many of those engaged in higher education) toward religious questions varies from casual disinterest to scrupulous avoidance. The reasons for this embarrassment are varied and sometimes well-intended. Clearly one's religion is ultimately a very personal matter. But this has often led to the false conclusion that religion ought never to reach the arena of public discussion. Admittedly, religion concerns matters that are not bound to the structures of reason. But all rational thinking, all inquiry about man and nature stems from fundamentally religious questions. Obviously, religion is a pluralistic human phenomenon, but this absence of consensus has led to the avoidance of efforts to deal forthrightly with the fundamental issues underlying all differences.

It must be acknowledged that the overreaction against religion has, no matter how understandable it has been, arisen out of experience. Persons can be hurt in the course of open exchanges of personal convictions, and there are ways in which the privacy of personal opinion can be violated. Religion has often been presented in ways that have done little credit to the ground rules of academic responsibility, and therefore have often won little academic respect. Furthermore, the pluralism of religious interpretation has made it frankly difficult to deal with religion in a manner pleasing to all segments of any community. Many dogmatic communities, then, have discouraged the campus from making any explorations at all into the deeper levels of religion. These facts underscore the difficulties of dealing with religious questions in the university, but they do not prove the impossibility or the inadvisability of it. The *manner* in which religion is dealt with on campus is crucial. It is not enough to plead for the enhancement of religion in the university without dealing with the manifold difficulties involved.

THE CONTRIBUTIONS AND LIMITATIONS OF THEOLOGY

Part of the problem at hand is semantic. It will be recalled that the earlier employment of Frankl's word "noetic" bore the advantage of a "non-specifically religious term," as Frankl says. It is the same non-specific sense of religion that is conveyed in the oft-encountered words "moral and spiritual values," which have arisen to avoid the embarrassment occasioned by the words "religion" and "religious." [7] In the last analysis, religion by any other name is still, as Paul Tillich asserts, man's "ultimate concern," and there may be as many reasons for the Christian to dismiss the word "religion" in favor of a more suitable one as to cling to it tenaciously.

Another ambiguous word is "theology," whose usefulness depends upon who is defining it. Robert Maynard Hutchins, in *The Higher Learning in America*, referred to theology in terms that are exceedingly restrictive, defining well enough the theology that characterized the medieval universities, but failing to appreciate the broader understandings of the true meaning of theology:

[7] It is noteworthy that the word "spiritual" rarely occurs unless accompanied by "moral" as a kind of anchor to keep "spiritual" from being swept into mystical spheres of connotation. In Frankl's writing, it is a way of assuring the translation of "spiritual" as "geistig" rather than "geistlich."

The medieval university had a principle of unity. It was theology. The medieval theologians had worked out an elaborate statement in due proportion and emphasis of the truths relating to man and God, man and man, and man and nature. It was an orderly progression from truth to truth. As man's relations to God were the highest of which he could conceive; as all his knowledge came from God and all his truths, the truths concerning God and man were those which gave meaning and sequence to his knowledge. Theology ordered the truths concerning man and man. . . . Theology ordered truths of man and nature.[8]

"But these are other times," Hutchins goes on to say in clear understatement. "Theology is banned by law from some universities. It might as well be from the rest." On the basis of the definition of theology with which Hutchins is working here we cannot but agree. With what follows, however, my entire thesis takes issue.

We are a faithless generation and take no stock in revelation. Theology implies orthodoxy and an orthodox church. We have neither. To look to theology to unify the modern university is futile and vain.[9]

Niebuhr has pointed out, however:

In the spotted reality of the medieval world it was not theology that governed the universities; it was rather the highly visible church. . . . It is also forgotten that theology no less than other human inquiries was in servitude then; and that when the great emancipation took place theology no less than humanistic studies and natural science participated in the revolt.[10]

With Niebuhr's help I have tried to say that faith is not reserved for theologians and revelation is by no means the church's monopoly. Faith is essential for and integral to all living, describes the context of all knowing and motivates all

[8] *The Higher Learning in America* (New Haven: Yale University Press, 1936), p. 96.
[9] *Ibid.,* p. 97.
[10] "Theology in the University," *Radical Monotheism,* p. 94.

doing, whether that of the physician, the politician, or the scholar. Revelation is an element in all history, personal and communal, religious and academic. The "theology" which Hutchins understands is the theology of a *department* rather than a *dimension* of human life. Professor Hutchins' argument has disqualified orthodoxy as a unifying instrument in the university, but it has not eliminated theology as a relevant dimension of academic pursuit.

The Harvard report, *The Objectives of General Education in a Free Society*,[11] similarly rejects theology as being no longer capable of serving as the foundation of the academic enterprise, which, due to its pluralism and its marked inner controversy, has no need of service from a body of conviction even more marked with pluralism and inner controversy. Yet this very Harvard report is shot through with religious implication which, for all its insistence on speaking in purely humanistic terms, raises inescapable issues of ultimate value, commitment, responsibility, and meaning within the context of faith. The report rightly refuses authority to "a theology," but in its effort to delineate the fundamental beliefs of man as the structure in which the academic enterprise can take place, the report is an exceedingly theological document.[12]

Hence it becomes clear that the word "theological" can be as variously employed and as easily misunderstood as the word "spiritual." And it is not only those who depreciate theology who tend to confine it to a restrictive understanding; those who appreciate it often do the same.

The notion of strengthening the theological aspects of a university may be understood by some to mean principally the addition of theologically trained men to the faculty. But

[11] (Cambridge: Harvard University Press, 1945). This 267-page report is now in its 18th printing.

[12] President Truman's Commission on Higher Education, issuing their report, *Higher Education for American Democracy* (New York: Harper & Bros., 1948), makes no mention of religion or theology. They offer, as the focus for American higher education, education for democracy, international understanding, and practical social objectives. In so doing, however, they make democracy a religion in the henotheistic sense.

these are not enough. Niebuhr[13] has described certain specifically "religious" schools with which he is familiar in terms much like those with which we became acquainted in our initial chapters. He reports that these schools have been marked by "multiplicity and indefiniteness of purpose" and a "lack of a sense of direction." Their curricula, though "more unified than most college curricula, are . . . nonetheless . . . a collection of studies rather than . . . a course of study." Their disunity, he says, "is also indicated in the efforts that are made to provide for 'integration' by adding examinations, theses or interdepartmental courses which will insure that students will combine in their own minds what has been fragmentarily offered them." These schools "have no clear conception of what they are doing . . . making separate responses to various pressures exerted by churches and society, contriving easy compromises among many values." These schools which Niebuhr was describing were graduate theological seminaries! Nevertheless, Niebuhr's observations illustrate that the mere presence of "theology" on the campus, in course descriptions or academic titles, does not immunize the school or the student from the loss of that dimension in education for which we have been grieving. Neither theological control nor theological content is enough to meet the challenge of education's ills. Rather, if we keep Frankl's image of the total dimensionality of man before us, we are likely to have a more responsible understanding of the meaning of theology, in the sense that Niebuhr uses the word, and thus a more accurate appreciation for the role that true theology plays in the life of the university.

Theology concerns the dimension in which is to be found that transcendent responsibility which a university accepts to "try to understand what is true for all men everywhere in the universal community and to communicate the truths it understands without bearing false witness against any neighbors." [14] Niebuhr carries his definition further. Theology concerns

---

[13] *The Purpose of the Church and Its Ministry* (New York: Harper and Bros., 1956), pp. 95, 97, 99, and 101.

[14] "Theology in the University," *Radical Monotheism*, p. 96.

that dimension in which resides "the confidence that the nature of things is such that bias, deceit, and falsehood, issuing from individual and social self-interestedness, cannot in any long run—in the final judgment, so to speak—triumph over honesty and rigorous self-discipline in study and communication." Theology, he goes on, concerns that dimension which deals with the "intellectual love of all truth in God, . . . an intellectual hope of salvation from error and falsehood as well as from ignorance." [15] Theology, as that which concerns the nature of the ultimate and man's relation to it, is intrinsic to the highest functions of the university. Theology, then, refers not exclusively to the God of the Old and New Testaments, but to all those objective beings which serve as objects of faith, centers of value, and bestowers of meaning. It is as universal a fact of man's life and reason as is the "metaphysics" which Hutchins proposes, but it entails an honest acknowledgment of the phenomena of faith and revelation (which are involved in the response of all men to the objects of their faiths).

Religion, therefore, is never brought to a campus nor theology added to an academic enterprise. Theological presuppositions are implicit in every intellectual undertaking as surely as faith is a reality of some kind in the life of every person and community. What is called for in our time, what is urgent if universities and their constituents are to be set on a more productive course toward the recovery of meaning, is not the external imposition of some foreign ingredient but the recognition and conscious ordering of a reality already present. It is not the invention of some new system we seek, or the spiritualization of education, but the recovery of full dimensionality in which, alone, a self or a university is whole.

Speaking of the individual self, Viktor Frankl refers to the "spiritual unconscious" which resides in each person and cries to be reawakened. A paraphrase of this term suggests the task at hand for those who would recover meaning in the

[15] *Ibid.*, pp. 96-97.

university: the illumination of the lost dimension requires the recovery of the "theological unconscious."

THE RECOVERY OF THE THEOLOGICAL UNCONSCIOUS

It was Sigmund Freud who first popularized the discovery that man's mind is largely beneath the conscious level. The "pre-conscious" can be recalled with effort, but beneath that lies the "dynamic unconscious," stored with all manner of thoughts and memories which are retrieved only with special efforts, usually requiring some kind of formal therapy. The dynamic behind the mind's tendency to assign certain thoughts and memories to the unconscious is complex, but generally has to do with fear, guilt, or some other threatening association. And no end of emotional energy, Freud told us, can be expended in keeping the lid on this Fibber McGee closet of hidden reflections. The recovery of this unconscious, or certain facets of it, is advisable in the interest of enhancing internal integrity and the freedom of conscious choices.

In spite of the essentially "religious" nature of the fundamental objectives of the university, in spite of the ineradicable presence of theological realities in the academic enterprise, in spite of the innumerable times that we are brought to the very threshold of this awareness by affirmations of faith, like those quoted earlier, which scrupulously avoid "religious" language, we retreat time and again from forthright acknowledgment and relegate the ultimate realities to the "theological unconscious" of academe. Some of the reasons for this repression have already been noted—human pride, academic totalitarianism, previous experience of autocratic ecclesiastical control, interpersonal insensitivity, not to mention certain practical and political influences, such as the constitutional provision for separation of church and state and the ticklish problem of maintaining the support of a religiously and anti-religiously pluralistic society. But for whatever the avowed reasons, the relegation of essential noetic considerations to the collective campus unconscious does to the university just what repression does to the potential mental patient: it buries under much camouflage the true sources of his illness, as well as his potential for greater wholeness.

It is all well and good to articulate the problem of the "theological unconscious" on the campus, but what, in fact, can be done about it? Given a particular academic mysteryhouse, how do its residents go about trying to discern some sensible design in its already chaotic pattern? How does such a pluralistic community as a university arrive at anything like a consensus of ultimate loyalty? In the face of the "many selves" that comprise any campus, can one ever hope to devise a commonly accepted standard from which all subsequent actions and decisions may be evaluated?

The first thing to be said in answer is that the task of recovery is as individual and induplicable an undertaking for each campus as it is for each person. There are no formulas to be given universal application. There are no loaded questions to which we await the "correct" answers. The theological unconscious of one academic community may disclose material quite different from that revealed by a neighboring college, or even a very similar one across the country. It is likely, therefore, that the strategies involved in the recovery process will extend beyond any generalizations that can be listed here.

Nevertheless, recovery will always involve at least three undertakings. The first is a matter of community memory, the second a reconsideration of already articulated commitments, and the third, a translation of all these commitments into expressions of universal concern, which will thereby become the unifying principle of the university as a whole.

A College's Faithful Remembering

Man is not the only creature with a memory, but he is the only *meaning-creating* creature, in whom memory plays an important part in the discernment of meaning. Of special importance among man's remembered experiences are those which have somehow illumined the rest of his experience and have lent to a total sense of identity. I have spoken of these experiences, following Richard Niebuhr, as "revelatory," suggesting that a person does not have to be a mystic, nor does a university have to be a church, in order for revelation to be a fact of their lives.

The recovery of the theological unconscious begins with total recall of the university's revelatory experiences. I indicated earlier what some of these might be—a moment of corporate victory on the ballfield or collective creativity on the stage, the graduation of a severely handicapped student or the involvement in the life of the surrounding city. Running deeper than any of these might be certain major kinds of activities or critical events which stand out in the campus memory.

Genuine revelation is, of course, not invented or selected. We can plan and bring about significant moments, but revelation is not planned; it happens. It is "given." However, a corporate examination of significant happenings by way of such questions as, "What events do you think most nearly revealed what our college is for?" or, "What experiences have best expressed the nature of our campus as a particular community?" would bring forth some revealing (!) observations.

The three results of recalling revelatory moments, it may be remembered, are: (1) to disclose patterns of cohesion in a varied past; (2) to bring into recollection those elements of the past which a college might prefer to forget, in which ideals were not lived up to, or principles of academic freedom or human sensitivity were violated; and (3) to open to its own view the past of other communities as well which might mean that the university would broaden its understanding of other institutions of society, including other universities, and determine its appropriate relationship to them.

In what sense does such review of revelatory episodes expedite a recovery of the theological unconscious? If by theology we mean a perception of those objective beings which serve as objects of faith, centers of value, and bestowers of meaning, then it might do this: A remembering of those most important occasions and events of the past would disclose what, in fact, has served as the center of value for a given campus over the years, or what has provided a center from which the campus has departed from time to time. Revelation, says Niebuhr, provides moments "when we are given a new faith to cleave to and to betray, a new standard to follow and to deny." [16] Experiences recollected from the past, in other words, will disclose what has been tacitly accepted as ultimate in the experience of the given university, and will thereby make explicit what have been its latent or unconscious objects of response. Thus by a faithful remembering of the significant past, the unconscious theological presuppositions of the college are recovered.

An appreciation of a community's history by no means suggests a bondage to that history. But an understanding and acceptance of the past is a necessary prelude to any reformation. A church-related college, for example, is "caught between its sectarian past and its public present," according to Charles S. McCoy, who asserts that a return to the sectarian past would be lethal to most such colleges and a dubious contribution to the current scene. But he also insists that an appreciation of its past commitments is necessary if it is to act responsibly in terms of its public present.[17]

Not many will be impressed by the importance of "faithful remembering." The past is what we're trying to get away from; some of it we are trying specifically to forget. That's what repression is all about. It is the future that concerns us more. And of all those comprising current campuses, those least likely to be excited by a review of the past are students. In contrast to an old song that declares, "I'd give a million tomorrows for just one yesterday," today's youth are more inclined to trade all the yesterdays for one good today. What has always been somewhat true of the young is now very markedly so: They seem to care altogether about the present, much less about the future, and not at all about the past. Witness the traditional ceremonies, the sentimental times of

---

[16] *The Meaning of Revelation*, p. 313.
[17] *New Identity for the Church-Related College* (book forthcoming).

remembering that bring tears to the eyes of the alumni and boredom to the faces of the young.

Unexciting as the past may seem to some, the fact remains that meaningful life is inseparable from both past and future, both history and goal. The past sheds needed light on questions of identity and purpose, and until some sense of community and personal history is recaptured, and some eye to the future is opened, meaning in the present will remain shallow and elusive. A sense of meaning does not come without some tedium, perhaps even boredom, and the act of faithful remembering, however unexciting it may seem to the Now Generation, is part of the price of the recovery of meaning in life.

A College's Corporate Commitment

The problems of arriving at anything like a consensus regarding a focus of responsibility would appear to be insurmountable. Even apart from such issues as church-state separation, the sheer size and pluralism of institutions, both public and private, militate against a simple achievement of corporate agreement. How, in any university of two to ten thousand, let alone in a multiversity of fifteen to thirty thousand, could one ever hope to come to a universally accepted decision? There is no evidence today that a church-related college of two thousand comes appreciably closer to achieving an overall perspective than state schools of many thousands.

Still and all, no university is presently without its affirmations of faith. Not only were corporate commitments publicly articulated and permanently recorded at the time of the founding and chartering of any institution, but they have been cautiously rehearsed ever since in such isolated moments of celebration as Founders' Days and Commencements. These commitments comprise part of the theological history of the institution. An examination of the charters and anniversary declarations of many of our major secular institutions might reveal unabashed expressions of radical monotheism in terms so specific as to bring considerable embarrassment to the church-state separatists on the campus.

Blowing the dust from the historic affirmations of the given university is suggested, therefore, as another step in the recovery of the theological unconscious. Such investigations may disclose what, at least at one time, was thought to provide the reason for that university's coming into being. Today, if a college is concerned to have more reason for being than simply to accommodate the growing number of high school graduates, it would do well to revisit its own faith affirmations. In so doing it may find that former assertions are no longer valid in their present form; nevertheless, taking original faith affirmations as a starting point, a given academic community may reexamine its commitment and consciously redefine it. If the school does not find it easy to arrive at an answer, it is at least prodded to ask the right question, the theological question: What is of ultimate importance to this community? What do we conceive to be "the Third beyond all our thirds," the ultimate object of response to which we owe loyalty and which should determine the general direction of all our decisions?

Calling a college campus to this kind of self-examination is like inviting a person to therapy; resistance will be maximum. Yet if our universities are genuinely ill, this is what is needed —not simply a single office call, but extended analysis. When representative selves of the campus gather—faculty, students, administrators, and trustees—to consider, over an extended period of time, the kinds of questions raised here, the resulting process will be as painful as it is productive. The interaction of perspectives and convictions and memories will reveal the same kind of schizophrenic disintegration that is present in the seriously disturbed psyche, and the patient will make every effort to avoid the painful process, but he cannot achieve integrity without it.

To be sure, there are some colleges who do not have the inner resources, the communal "ego strength," the sheer daring to undertake such a recovery process. These will be the

colleges and universities that will make no appreciable headway toward the solution of the crisis of meaninglessness.

A College's Breadth of Concern

Throughout these pages I have echoed the words of those
who have asserted the importance of some kind of "transcendent dimension" in higher education which may help to
bring a needed synthesis to the whole academic enterprise. I
have gone on to say that this dimension does not call for
construction, but for *recovery,* and that therefore each individual university that wishes to come to terms with its
fundamental problem has some remembering to do, some
faith affirmations to rediscover in the interest of determining
what it conceives to be ultimate and worthy of its total response. It must choose what cause is qualified to serve as the
final object of the varied and complex triadic responses that
characterize the particular university.

Yet still we cannot help asking if such an objective is at
all realistic. How does a community achieve consensus when
it is fundamental to the very nature of that community to be
pluralistic, to specialize in the engagement of many varieties
of perspectives, thus serving as a kind of "theological marketplace"? Ernest Becker has high hopes for the university's
becoming the seat of a new Moral View of the world.
"Imagine," he dreams, "the university teaching the right, a
right so unmistakable as to be worth potentially the sacrifice
of a life!" But Becker is not so naïve as this sentence would
suggest. He continues: "The anguished question remains:
How can we get agreement on what to promote—how *do* we
promote human value?" [18]

It would appear that the task is futile—but if it is, and if
my thesis is correct, then the quest for meaning is futile, and
there is little that can be done to solve the problem that so
many have identified for so long as the central problem of the
university and the selves who comprise it.

Need we despair so quickly? Pluralistic societies have

[18] *Beyond Alienation,* p. 112.

been known to embrace certain common ideals in spite of radical differences of understanding. Certain tacitly accepted presuppositions (such as the knowability of the universe and the goodness of truth) already characterize every university. A more far-removed but useful illustration of pluralism within a mutual commitment is seen in the figure of Alcoholics Anonymous, a widely divergent fellowship of persons of many ages and situations, backgrounds and interests, but sharing two things in common: a problem honestly confessed and an *ultimate* openly acknowledged. This *ultimate* is the agreed-upon object of their ultimate responsibility and the ultimate source of their aid, but never the subject of forced consensus. The commonly accepted theological reference in "AA" circles is "God, as I understand Him."

Without pushing the figure a bit further, I submit that this is the style of understanding appropriate for the university seeking the recovery of the lost dimension. The ultimate may be given many names. For most, except for the professional theologian or the metaphysician, the term "Being Itself" is too esoteric to be helpful, and to many the term "God" is associated with too narrow a concept. A consensus regarding the name of the ultimate will not be forthcoming on most campuses, and it does not need to be. For the naming of it is not the issue. What is the issue is the implications which this ultimate holds for the responses of the university. The principle of radical monotheism suggests a radical concern for universal community, and this, as the rediscovered affirmations of faith will generally disclose, is not far removed from the articulated concerns expressed by most institutions of higher learning.

Most universities worthy of the name will publicly assert that their reason for being extends far beyond the confines of the campus, even beyond the borders of the state. Although the surrounding tax-paying, gift-giving society may not always understand all the ways in which the college serves their broader interests, the persons who founded the school often claimed to understand them, and all the commencement addresses and catalog prefaces are variations on the same theme, namely, that institutions of higher learning are not built simply to produce teachers and businessmen, doctors and coaches, and not just to prepare citizens of the state, but to produce servants of mankind and citizens of the world, prepared to engage in the great issues of the day. In spite of the occasional denominational jealousy or excessive vocationalism or sheer community pomposity that motivated the establishment of some of our colleges, the average school, in her better moments, does not see herself within any narrow state, denominational or even national frame of reference. Rather, she extends her verbalized concern to the world at large. She may even, during lapses in her secular propriety, make passing references to God.

On the face of it at least, higher education has long expressed its concern for universal community. With some regularity it has come close to espousing (at least for the public) the principle of radical monotheism. However, it is not on the level of articulations that we have our trouble. It is on the level of practical decisions, of living out an actual life-style of the campus. As Emerson would put it, what we do speaks so loudly that people cannot hear what we say. And among those who have the greatest difficulty hearing what their colleges are saying are the students!

What I am arguing for is a more explicit expression, a more consistent loyalty, a more unapologetic affirmation of the conviction that *there is something written into the nature of ultimate reality that calls for concern for universal community*. If this were our unifying principle, all decisions could be made, all values measured, and all responses formulated in terms of that central concern.

I stop short of calling the goal "Ultimate Concern," for that would imply that universal community itself is another god. Henotheism, as we have seen, is that social faith which makes a finite society the object of ultimate trust and loyalty. Universal concern is not a god; it is an *implication* of God (God in the largest sense). In point of fact, concern for the well-being of universal community may be interpreted from a primarily humanistic point of view, or from a biblical perspective, or from some other theistic understanding. In any case it is theological in the sense of being a conception of what is ultimate. The specific interpretation of this must be left to the given university as surely as to the individual self. Let it simply be said that if a university cannot embrace loyalty to the *Source of being*, or at least to universal community, then it must not wonder at the unrelenting persistence on its campus of the meaning problem in all its modes. My contention remains: The depth and duration of meaning in the self and in the life of a community, vary directly with the magnitude and ultimacy of the object to which commitment is made.

However, the theological unconscious is not awakened by speculation or memory alone, nor is it brought to life simply by the armchair formulation of a corporate commitment. Meaning is not revealed by formulas or contained in ideas. It is disclosed in a process, the process being best described as a response of existential commitment. Truth, in the final analysis, must be *done*. Commitment to the well-being of universal community means involvement in universal community. Meaning is not recovered simply by identifying the appropriate object of response, but by responding, by living out that which is implied by the commitment. Just as the healthy self "comes to itself" in the intercourse of its everyday relationships with other selves, so the university will ultimately realize its full dimensional identity in the course of its engagement with the world.

The university has, of course, always engaged in and responded to the realities that surrounded it on one level or another, the realities of either the natural world or the social milieu. The training of business and professional people, engagement in scientific research, the provision of special consultants for local and national problems and the offering of cultural events for the surrounding community—all are instances of community involvement. But for the most part, the university has been far less creative in its responses than it could be. Our responses have been primarily reflective rather than active, technological more than social, and more transmissive than critical. The major role of university involvement has been that of training persons for future interaction while discouraging engagement in present interaction. To be involved in these limited ways has meant inadequate involvement, and thus irrelevance.

INVOLVEMENT REVISITED

If a university is to discover the source of its meaning by way of increased involvement in the well-being of universal community, it must at the same time guard against the reductionist fallacy of politicalization or activism. The university can appropriately play its role as an agent of social change only if it carefully recalls its *primary* function as that of intellectual inquiry. But the importance of its primary roles provides no justification for slighting its secondary roles.

The manner in which this increased involvement and actualized concern for universal community will be spelled out must, as I have indicated, be the unique assignment of each institution, but in no instance will the task be undertaken adequately without attention to at least three specific enterprises which have been implied by all that has preceded in our discussion: (1) provision for participatory governance by a broader spectrum of the entire university community; (2) a fearless reevaluation of the present nature and style of involvement of the university in the larger society; (3) the development of what Paul Denise has called the "paracurriculum."

Participation in University Governance

If the university is to be thought of as an answering agency, much student clamor these days can be understood as appeals for the opportunity to help shape the answers, which in turn will enable the students to fulfill their human calling as answering selves. Students are not the only ones who cry for this. An even older battle has been waged on many campuses by faculty for participation in decisions relating to matters not exclusively academic, such as the design of campus buildings, the participation of the institution in extra-campus affairs, and the general ordering of priorities among college concerns. Charles S. McCoy has declared that "college governance may be at the root of the problem of meaning," and that the time has come to move from a "center of authority" to a "community of authority" on campus.[19] Although he addresses himself specifically to the church-related college, his insight is no less valid for other institutions willing to confront the problem of meaninglessness by the avenue of responsibility. No longer can the categories of responsibility be so neatly distributed among the components of a college— the trustees being responsible for ultimate policy decisions, the administration for executing these policies, the faculty for teaching, and the students for learning. While the emphasis may still be appropriate in each case, the lines cannot be so tightly drawn. The responsibilities of imparting, appropriating, directing, and implementing in the university must be jointly exercised. A radical reappraisal of the structures of governance is, therefore, a priority need on most campuses.

Evaluation of the School's Involvement in the Larger Society

This total community of authority must undertake a bold and thorough reevaluation of the university's present participation in the life of the world, both at local and more far-reaching levels. It is against the ideal of responsibility for the well-being of universal community that the school's involvement must be measured. A university's service endeavors, its financial investments, its research projects, its scholarship programs must all fall under this scrutiny.

Of course no university can serve all publics. One college cannot literally increase the well-being of the entire human population. But a given institution can determine how to assist in meeting the needs of a limited public in a manner that at least does not militate against the well-being of universal community.

It is not difficult to understand why some students and

[19] *New Identity for the Church-Related College* (book forthcoming).

professors today see a gross inconsistency between the commitments to the betterment of mankind which their school professes, and its simultaneous assistance in developing nationalistic systems of weaponry. It is extremely difficult to reconcile military research and development with the fundamental purposes of higher education or the good of universal community. Whatever the rationale for maintaining a strong military defense, whatever the argument for its place in the purposes of universal peace, the issue is that of the appropriateness of the university's commitment to the military task. The senior editor of *Look* magazine has put it quite bluntly:

> If U.S. colleges and universities want to stay in touch with the best of the new generation of students—and end campus violence —they will simply have to renounce all connection with military research and development. War work is an inappropriate and corrupting activity for an institution of higher education. Other institutions can examine their own consciences.[20]

Whether a given university concurs with this judgment or not, it must at least review its basis for judgment on the matter. It should also understand why, as a campus, it presumes to prepare students in one building to bring healing to human tensions, while developing chemical warfare agents in the next building. Its failure to understand and discuss its own commitments in this area has created an atmosphere among many of its members of ultimate frustration and meaninglessness.

The Paracurriculum

Under similar scrutiny by the whole campus community must come the total curriculum and extracurriculum of the university. But a further and especially creative facet of the curriculum bears examination and expansion; that is the area of opportunities for constructive and educative community

[20] George B. Leonard, "Beyond Campus Chaos," *Look*, June 6, 1969, p. 78.

involvement which parallels the standard curriculum and which, therefore, has been called the paracurriculum." [21] Included here is a broad range of living-learning experiences that supplement the formal learning context. They extend far beyond the level of private tutoring and park recreation assistance, although these are valid beginnings for the kind of person-to-person involvement called for. The paracurriculum challenges virtually every department of the college to create opportunities for applying what is learned on the campus to what is presently encountered in the world.

Sociology students, for instance, under faculty leadership and with local community cooperation, may undertake studies useful to a Mayor's Committee on Human Relations or a city council, or a city-county planning board. They may assist in providing "family services" or assist the staffs of hospitals, homes, or community centers. Business majors might devise ways to help lower income people to plan budgets or start businesses, or they might organize data concerning the economic problems of a locale. Physical science students could pursue specific research projects aimed at serving human need, such as air and water pollution control, medical drug control, and agricultural development. Or consider the possibility of art majors and physical education majors combining forces and talents to offer "creativity workshops" for the community at large. Or reflect on the potential among students of psychology and the communication arts for the joint programming of a "communications experiment" for groups of mixed ages or cultures for the purpose of interpreting and overcoming the generation gap or other forms of human estrangement.

The possibilities challenge the imagination, and if the examples given here seem superficial, they need only to be supplanted by more carefully studied projects which are uniquely relevant to a specific situation. The idea of integral community involvement is not new, but it is rare. Striking

[21] Paul Denise, "The Prophetic Microcosm and the Paracurriculum," *Yankee Student Opinion*, February 1965.

illustrations can be found, however, in several colleges. A few of these schools require at least one such activity of each student for graduation. Experimentation with paracurriculum will not be without its problems. While some of these activities will help to break down certain barriers between town and gown, others may sow suspicions and generate hostility, which presents obvious public relations problems for the college.[22] Some projects will be rewarding to students while others may be depressing and discouraging. But the paracurriculum will have the long-run effect of making study courses more relevant, building bridges of correlation between them, providing avenues of "now-response" to the world that is, and in that way conferring meaning on both the individual and the community.

The import of the last several pages has been that the theological unconscious of a university will be recovered not only as the past is remembered, but as the present is restructured; not only as commitments are reformulated, but as they are acted out in fresh new ways. The concern underlying all this is not only that the larger society today is in desperate

[22] Problems of public relations provide further illustration of the need for a "community of authority" for working through the decisions that face a divided campus. This community should not exclude public relations and development officers. Academicians, particularly the socially sensitive ones, it seems, frequently overlook the fact that *timing* is one of the critical factors in any decision for change. Though timing is, of course, a concern for others than public relations people, it presents special problems for the college that is heavily dependent on the whims of a gift-giving public. Certain college activities and pronouncements which are appropriate to the responsibilities of a university could, at the wrong time, utterly disrupt some proximate objective of the college. On the other hand, attention to timing does represent a form of compromise, and while the radically idealistic among students and faculty may view compromise as inconsistent and immoral, the ultimately responsible member of society must view it as a political reality. Timing with an eye to public response does not *necessarily* violate loyalty to a conviction. For an administrative office to suggest a better time for a certain move and give reasons for the suggestion is to make a useful contribution to the discernment of appropriate response. For such an office to say, "Do not do or say this at all," or to procrastinate without reason, is only to widen the communication gap.

need of the talents and creativity available in universities, but that the sense of meaning on the part of selves and communities is at stake. Both facts call for a revisit to responsibility as the principal gateway to meaning. The recovery process outlined above will be difficult and time-consuming, threatening to certain accustomed patterns and painful to certain cherished preconceptions. But it will be optional only to those who are not yet persuaded of the unavoidable relationships between meaning and responsibility. The recovery process will be unessential only to those who believe that meaning is not, after all, the critical dimension of education or of life, the ultimate quest of thoughtful selves and communities.

HUMANIZING THE UNIVERSITY

The title of the present chapter, "The Faith of a Secular University," appears to be a misnomer. In discussing the inescapability of religion and proposing the necessity of a recovery of the theological unconscious, no mention whatever has been made of the secular. The omission is intentional because any distinction between sacred and secular is deceptive. But now we must turn to the meaning of the secular with respect to the university, which, I have contended, needs urgently to recover its religious dimension.

Secularization is by no means a new phenomenon. In the book which has done most to bring the subject to public attention, *The Secular City,* Harvey Cox traces the process of secularization to biblical roots. Before Cox, the German theologian Friedrich Gogarten, whose thought pioneered the modern day "theology of the secular," maintained that secularization is the logical consequence of the impact of biblical faith upon history.

While the phenomenon itself is not new, massive attention to it is, and one cannot understand the university of the seventies apart from some familiarity with the process and meaning of secularization. Secularization has been variously defined, but all discussions reflect at least four common motifs of secularization which are so closely related as to be almost four ways of saying the same thing.[23]

The first is *a fundamental concern for this world.* In theology this is expressed in a reaction against an "otherworldly" focus of former years. The word "secular" is derived from the Latin *saeculum,* "world" or "age" which early Christians began to interpret as "this world" or "this age" as opposed to some other world or later age. Secularization, then, is the unapologetic emphasis upon the present world with all its needs, possibilities, and limitations. It is a renunciation of inaction in the name of waiting for a supernatural power; it is also a rediscovery of the biblical notion that it is this world in which God acts and for which God harbors an unmeasured concern. Secularization, by this token, is essentially sacrilegious only to those to whom some other age or world is more important than the present one.

A second and related theme is *the evaporation of firm boundaries between the sacred and the secular.* Following logically from the notion that the present world is the domain of God and the arena of his action, any identification of certain buildings or hours, activities, persons or books, as uniquely sacred is called into radical question. H. Richard Niebuhr has been quoted earlier[24] as having proclaimed that the principle of radical monotheism makes all things secular, and at the same time sanctifies all things, since all things come from God. The world itself is sacred. So Bonhoeffer speaks of a "holy worldliness," and Bishop John A. T. Robinson calls for "worldly holiness." Moreover, the institutions within the world which claim a particular religious function and sacred responsibility do, in fact, share in the world's profaneness. The line can no longer be drawn between sacred and secular.[25]

[23] The book *Secularization and the University,* by Harry E. Smith (Richmond: John Knox Press, 1968), has been helpful to me in this discussion.

[24] Chap. III, pp. 91-92.

[25] It is in the context of this disdain for the isolation of the holy that current notes of anti-clericalism must be understood: not in the sense of general opposition to the importance of the church and the value of its

A third theme is that of *pluralism and the dissolution of a sense of wholeness.* This refers not only to religious pluralism which is coming to have such an effect on legal interpretations of religious freedom in our country, but it has to do with the disappearance of any prevailing sense of cohesion and orderliness which has so long been characteristic of Western thought. It involves the loss of any single, overarching world view, whether that of divine determinism or of scientific orderliness. It is the growing recognition that there are many different perspectives from which reality may be viewed, and a variety of ultimate commitments. In writing on *The Idea of a Secular Society,* D. L. Munby lists certain characteristics of such a society:

> (a) A secular society is one which explicitly refuses to commit itself as a whole to any particular view of the nature of the universe and the place of man in it. . . .
> (b) Such a society is unlikely to be homogeneous and we do not find homogeneity. . . . A secular society is in practice a pluralistic society, insofar as it is truly secular.[26]

A fourth theme in discussions of secularization is the *emphasis upon modern man's new responsibility.* Harvey Cox has spoken of secularization as a "process of maturing and assuming responsibility. . . ." He charges that "man must now assume responsibility for his own world. He can no longer shove it off on some religious power." This new depth of responsibility is brought about in part by the development of natural science which has freed man from a superstitious dependence upon and bondage to the world.

So Friedrich Gogarten says: "The decisive thing is that modern man is no longer responsible to the world and its power as the classical man and, in a modified way, even the medieval man was. Instead he has become the one who is re-

---

ministry, but in the sense of denying any superiority to ordained ministry and ecclesiastical institutions.

    [26] *The Idea of a Secular Society* (London: Oxford University Press, 1963), pp. 14, 17.

sponsible *for* his world." [27] Bonhoeffer describes responsibility in this "world come of age" in terms of "deputyship" in which "man is directly obliged to act in the place of other men." Again the thrust of secularization is opposed to waiting for supernatural intervention, and stresses human response to what is taking place.

These four motifs, then, are at the heart of the process of secularization which, the newer theologians are saying, should not be viewed as the enemy of biblical faith, but as its natural consequence and as a development to be appreciated and strengthened by Jews and Christians. Yet the process is by no means an unmixed blessing, for it is susceptible, like all processes of history, to corruption. The tentative and relative perspectives of secularity may somehow become absolutized; the openness to pluralistic variety can become a new kind of closedness; the focus on the present world can become a purely horizontal consideration, devoid once again of the vertical "depth" dimension. Then, as many have suggested, secularization becomes secularism.

This brief and superficial excursus into the meaning of secularization should disclose that a good college or university is, by definition, thoroughly secular. This is less obviously true with respect to certain of the four themes than to others. Let us reexamine the four motifs of secularization in reverse order: responsibility, pluralism, the waning cleavage between sacred and secular, and worldly concern.

Responsibility is, of course, the key concept of the present study. Essentially my message has been that responsibility is the key to the discovery of meaning in life and that the "relative ultimacy" of one's object of response will largely determine the "relative sufficiency" of one's derived sense of meaning. Secularization's renewed focus on human responsibility tends to undergird my thesis: that man come of age is man-the-answerer and that the university come of age, the authentically secular university, is a university that under-

<hr />

[27] *The Reality of Faith,* trans. Carl Michalson *et al.* (Philadelphia: Westminster Press, 1959), p. 168.

stands itself to be a responding agency, responding consciously to the highest possible object of response. The *pluralism* of a good college or university is assumed, and has been well rehearsed here. The campus is a marketplace of perspectives and hence, in this sense too, a secular community. One may appropriately inquire again how the essentially pluralistic university relates to my proposal for an ultimate focus of responsibility. How can a genuine university orient itself around a common concern for the good of universal community without jeopardizing its "authentic secularity" which requires that it eschew all overarching world views? Chapter III emphasized that pluralism is not itself the culprit on campus. It is not loyalty to several causes that marks our irresponsibility, but ultimate loyalty to what are, in reality, penultimate causes. It is not an overarching world view on the part of a given university that is being called for, but regard for a principal focus of concern. It is not Becker's plea for a New Moral View of the World that is being ordered, but an appropriate common denominator that provides a basic unifying principle for the proliferated tasks of the university. Although Munby declares that "a secular society is one that explicitly refuses to commit itself to any particular view of the nature of the universe," he goes on to say that "any society must have some common aim, in the sense that people are doing things together to produce certain effects." [28] It is the need for this kind of "common aim" on the part of an authentically secular university that, I suggest, calls for an ultimate focus of responsibility if not a generally accepted object of response, if the pluralism of the campus is not to become schizophrenia, and its fragmentation is not to result in ideological disintegration.

It is not so obvious that the *waning bifurcation between sacred and secular concerns* on the campus is a sign of healthy secularization. One is more inclined to see in this development a discouraging trend, evidenced by what appears to be a total elimination of religious perspectives and ecclesiastical

[28] *The Idea of a Secular Society*, p. 23.

control. While these results have certainly occurred in many cases, they do not represent what we mean by secularization; the genuinely secular university is not one in which the religious has been eliminated, but one in which false distinctions between sacred and secular have been broken down. In schools where this true secularization has taken place, religion has been relegated less and less to chapel and religion departments and embodied more and more as an integral dimension in the entire enterprise. To the extent that some universities, notably state schools, have eliminated religion from their total curricular and extracurricular considerations on campus, they have failed to be authentically secular, to educate the whole man, or in those other words, they have failed to *come of age*. This is by no means true of all state schools. We see some today making dramatic moves in the direction of incorporating explicitly religious considerations into both their curricular and extracurricular programs.

It must be clearly understood that the university that becomes secular in the true sense does not, by that token, become less religious, but on the contrary, is freed to become more genuinely religious. It is the college that fails to remember the tentativeness and relativity of all its perspectives and the openness to corruption of its own structures that falls into the snare of secularism, and thereby becomes *sacrilegious*. The more authentically secular a university becomes, the more genuinely religious; the more responsibly religious a school becomes, the more thoroughly secular.

We have real difficulty here with the word "religion" because religion has in fact, instead of "binding together" as the word suggests, too often tended to divide. We need to think of it now in terms of Frankl's "noetic dimension." However, perhaps a more useful distinction than either *secularization* or *noeticization* of the university is simply the *humanization* of the university. The truly secular and genuinely religious institution of higher learning will be the truly human university. Recall that the uniquely human being is a meaning-creating being, that the mature human being is a *responding* being, and that it is as responder or answerer, or as a member of a community of answerers, that man discerns meaning. Just as it is at the point where human responsibility is denied that secularization becomes secularism, it is at that same point that man and his institutions become less human, become, as we say, dehumanized. Thus, either a religious or an irreligious institution can ignore the student's need for response, and thereby become dehumanized or "secularistic."

Finally, that characteristic of true secularization having to do with *concern for this world* is an appropriate mark of a mature university. Were a university to retreat to an exclusive concern with philosophical speculation or historical reflection, were it even to study the present world, but with detachment and manifest unconcern, it would, to the measure of its separation, fail to be secular and fall short of being a university. The authentic university is the university intimately concerned with the world, with due attention to the involvement of past and future in the present.

Once again, to take the present seriously is to take full dimensionality seriously. As I have contended, the recovery of the noetic dimension enables fuller appropriation of the present. Our concern must be that the secular university not be without depth. The full and authentic secularity of that university, its humanness, requires a recovering of that depth dimension.

The scope of the task that confronts the modern university is captured in a challenge laid down by Walter Lippmann who emphasizes the ultimate inseparability of "worldly" and "spiritual" concerns. Writing on "The University and the Human Condition" Lippmann says,

> As men become modern men, they are emancipated and thus deprived of the guidance and support of traditional and customary authority. Because of this, there has fallen to the universities a unique, indispensable and capital function in the intellectual and spiritual life of modern society. I do not say that the universities today are prepared to perform this spiritual and intellectual function. What I do say is that a way will have to be found to perform these functions if the pursuit of the good life,

to which this country is committed, is to continue and to be successful. . . . The universities must fill the void because they alone can fill it.[29]

The task is, to say the least, a frightening one. Some universities will rise to the challenge, some will not. Which universities will be the responsive ones is impossible to predict. What is a certainty is that the universities that will be prepared to meet Lippman's challenge for total education will be those which are both authentically secular and profoundly religious.

[29] *The New Republic*, May 28, 1966, p. 17.

6

The period after the Civil War in the United States witnessed a great transformation from the age of the college to the age of the university. It was a process accompanied by a growing secularization of higher education. The higher learning and religious faith knew at best an uneasy truce; at worst they engaged in bitter and fruitless warfare. In a hundred years the ties of higher education and religion in the United States have largely been severed. Yet the relation has by no means been completely ended. The two institutions continue to share common concerns and to seek a basic unity in which knowledge and faith realize complementary rather than competing contributions to man's life.[1]

THE MINISTRY OF AND TO EDUCATION

We have been reminded *ad nauseam* that ours is an age of "marketing personalities," "organization men," and the "lonely crowd," an age when we have become so increasingly impersonal and detached that we see men "as trees walking," and we are making machines so human in their behavior that they seem almost like men thinking. This depersonalization has become true of our commonest relationships. As Edward Stein puts it, "A cashier becomes a hand with money; the clerk becomes a voice with answers, the wife becomes a cook with sex, the child becomes a nuisance with need." If the student, then, becomes little more than a source of tuition

[1] John D. Millett, *The Academic Community* (New York: McGraw-Hill, 1963), p. 38.

GOD SO LOVED THE UNIVERSITY

with a psychological problem, it is little wonder that he protests so vehemently this IBM-card style of uncommunity.

The condition is not likely to improve as our technology
grows more complex, nor is student protest against it likely
to subside, unless it disintegrates into despair. If we are
called, as some suggest, to celebrate our technology, we are
also called surely to be alert to its dehumanizing dangers. To
no one is this call more urgently addressed than to colleges
and universities. If schools of higher learning are to do more
than turn out the mechanics and servants of society, if they
are also to prepare human beings to be alert to human issues
and sensitive to human concerns, then personal concern must
itself be an ingredient in the learning context. Although a
college is not a hospital for the psychologically ill, it is a
training ground for psychological maturity and social sensitivity. Though it is not a finishing school for inculcating the
young with manners and etiquette, it is a laboratory for cul-
tivating moral responsibility. Those who are inclined to consider this the exclusive task of the church, the home, and the
Boy Scouts are oblivious to the full import of the kind of
spiritual task that has fallen to the university.

It is strange that we should be surprised to find ourselves
speaking of the objectives of the university in spiritual terms.
Throughout history, until the present century, the intellectual and spiritual aspects of public education have been
closely intertwined.

Whatever controversy may rage concerning the origins of
colleges, it is accurate to assert that the Christian church is
the mother of higher education in America. No doubt it was
not a virgin birth, but however one assigns the paternity of
higher education, the burden of the labor and nurture of the
earliest colleges and universities was largely that of the
church. Colonial colleges, though not always founded exclusively to train ministers, were founded by churchmen: Harvard and Yale by Congregationalists, Columbia and William
and Mary by Anglicans, Brown by Baptists, Princeton by
Presbyterians, and so forth.

To be sure, the church's nurture was characterized by

mixed identities. Sometimes her love was like that of a nig-
gardly stepmother. Other times it was smother-love. But the
preachers who administered the early American colleges and
comprised almost all their faculties had a devout (if not
always clear) vision of the church's responsibility to guide
the life of the mind.

The church's concern for higher education was not, of
course, born in colonial America. Though its history had been
marked by occasional moods of incipient anti-intellectualism
and all too often by a dogmatic authoritarianism, the church's
concern for higher education had been a dominant and sus-
taining force ever since Paul first carried the gospel of
Jerusalem to the scholarly community of Athens. From the
time of Clement and Augustine, through Thomas, Erasmus,
Luther, and Calvin to the present day, the church has pro-
duced outstanding scholars who have taken seriously the
biblical commission to "love God with the mind." While education was minimal during the Dark Ages, it was kept alive
largely by the church, in the form of monastic schools.
When universities came to be established it was the church
that provided the impetus and the leadership. The University
of Paris, founded about 1200 and destined to become the
pattern for the universities of the Middle Ages, was founded,
at least spiritually, by Peter Abelard. Although the Reformation loosened the grip of Catholicism on education, the interest of the churches in education was by no means diminished.
A striking illustration of Protestant regard for learning is the
impact of Puritanism upon education in Great Britain and,
even more, in America, an enthusiasm tempered only by a
steadfast refusal to invest ultimate trust in the minds of
men.

What is required in the present day, then, is not that the
church *develop* a concern for higher education but that she
forcefully recapture and *carefully update* a concern she has
almost always had. The kind of concern appropriate today is
entirely different from what was appropriate in the colonial
period and certainly in the days of the frantic founding of
denominational colleges. As we have observed, we have

entered upon an era marked by the collapse of much traditional religion on the one hand and a growing spiritual concern on the other. As Bonhoeffer has characterized it: "The world is more godless and nearer to God than ever before." Illustrative of this trend are such cogent spiritual analyses of our time as the one by Walter Lippmann that ended our last chapter, and that pointedly assigns the university an essentially spiritual function.

The church can respond to the assertion of this larger function of the university in one of two ways: either she can react in defensiveness with a kind of professional jealousy to what appears to be prideful usurpation of her own sovereign responsibility, or she can see the academic challenge as a task that calls for all the creative resources society can muster and for which the university will need responsible spiritual guidance. The latter response would call for the church to make a "third shift" in its philosophy of campus ministry.

Having moved gradually away from the parochial concept of higher education, universities in the first half of this century became the separated brother to whom the church ministered. "Foundations" were built alongside state campuses, or "Christian fellowships" were established on private campuses, like missions set up to win students to themselves. More recently, the emphasis has shifted to the concept of ministering *within* the university—a concept based on the axiom that the church exists wherever two or three are gathered together in his name.[2] By this understanding, a follower of Christ, whose patterns of thought and style of life are presumably shaped by his Christian commitment, may minister as he fulfills his responsibilities as a creative teacher or administrator, trustee or student. According to this view, the church is found where Christians are active, within the university or elsewhere.

But now a further shift in philosophy is called for which by no means abandons the notion of the church ministering within the university but goes beyond it. This philosophy

[2] Matthew 18:20.

acknowledges that, in truth, the creative task of the modern university is a ministry of its own. While it is not specifically a Christian ministry, yet, to the extent that it is concerned with human betterment, the discernment of the good and the true, and the human quest for meaning, it is an essential ministry to man's need and worthy of whatever assistance and support the church can give. By this understanding the church no longer relates itself to the university as its parent or its supervisor, but as a partner concerned with giving birth and strength to those movements and agencies in society that lend to the sanctification of life and the redemption of society.

Even the meaning of "church-related college" has had to be rethought within this framework. Increasingly we find denominational colleges, originally built and financed by the churches, undergoing charter revisions that reduce the required number of clerical or church-appointed trustees, and thus liberating the college from legal domination (church control) while assuring the continuation of the church's vital interest (church-relatedness). The value of this move is more than the practical advantage of increasing the college's eligibility for non-church financial support (which, undoubtedly, the college desperately needs). The more basic motivation involves the ultimate freedom of academic institutions to pursue their tasks without the restrictions, real or implied, of any controlling agency.

Church colleges of the past were frequently called "Christian colleges," a title that implied that the subjects in their curricula were taught from "a Christian point of view" and faculty were hired with particular reference to their religious affiliation. The fallacy of that approach lay in the implication, which too often became a conscious effort, that there could be taught a "Christian biology" as distinct from any other kind of honest study of biology, or a "Christian economics" or a "Christian U.S. history." Where this was tried, academic integrity often suffered at the hands of teachers who were better evangelists than they were academicians.

Freedom from domination by any single agency or ideology is important to any responsible college or university. The first appropriate concern of the Christian for higher education is not that universities be dominated by the church, but that universities be supported by the church, morally if not always financially, that the church do all in its power to help the university to be itself, free and uncontrolled by external agencies, and to help it become the best and most responsible educating force that it can be. The Christian's concern will not be so much that biology, economics, and history be taught by Christians as that they be taught by competent teachers. To be sure, he will also be concerned that the Christian perspective be given a fair, persuasive, and academically sound presentation at as many points as appropriate, not only in church-related colleges but in all accredited schools. The informed Christian is also concerned for other dimensions of the campus enterprise in addition to its scholastic pursuits: its extracurricular program, its community life style, the quality of its interpersonal relationships, and the nature of its involvement in the world.

As will become evident later in this chapter, the Christian churchman's concern for higher education does not terminate at the borders of the church-related college. But the subject of the church-affiliated college having been raised, it would be well to examine it at this point. A misreading of the growing process of secularization in our time could lead one to conclude that the future of the church-related college has been jeopardized. There are those in our time who believe this, who claim that the college that wishes to survive must minimize its church-relatedness. Notable among these are Jencks and Riesmann who have made a study of *The Academic Revolution.*

Warren Bryan Martin has declared that the church can no longer provide the ultimate focus for institutions of higher learning.[3] Harvey Cox made a stronger assertion in his earlier edition of *The Secular City,* in which he said the organizational church has no role on the campus and should stay out. In the Preface to his revised edition Cox modifies

---

[3] *Alternative to Irrelevance,* p. 138.

his position somewhat, attempting "to make it clear that it is not the organized church as such that is unwelcome in the university, but its institution-centered and imperialistic attitude." [4]

Virtually all educators agree that the university can no longer be an "arm of the church," that it must be independent of external control. What is not so clear is the position in which this leaves the church-related college, the role it is called to play, and whether, in fact, its relation to the church historically and presently is an asset or a liability. Let us pursue this question further.

THE PERILS AND POTENTIALS OF THE CHURCH-RELATED COLLEGE

There are no firm grounds for claiming the superiority of the church-related college. Many studies have disclosed that, on the whole, church-related colleges have tended toward the mediocre academically. While many do a better than average job in maintaining a style of community life, this reputation is not exclusively the claim of the church-related college. While some have undertaken innovative programs of various sorts, the reputation is more often that of imitating rather than initiating innovation.

Although the church college cannot claim superiority on any level, I contend that it does possess certain latent advantages which could serve to give it a marked head start in the critical task of ending irrelevance and restoring a sense of meaningfulness to higher education.

There are at least three such advantages that a church-related college may possess: (1) a heritage of human concern expressed both internally and externally; (2) a maximum openness to religious considerations; and (3) a theological framework of understanding which can provide illumination for the task of the humanizing university.

To note these potential advantages is in no way to suggest that colleges not related to the church are not marked by human concern, or that all religious considerations are absent

[4] P. xii.

there, or that such campuses are devoid of theologically sensitive persons and groups. Religion, as we have been discussing
it, cannot possibly be banned from any campus, either by law
or by charter provision. Theological presuppositions of some
kind (or several kinds) reside in the theological unconscious
of every university. Human concern is, one would hope, a
characteristic of all human communities, to some degree. But
while I do not speak here of characteristics unique to the
church-related college, I do see them as distinct advantages
in these schools. What may be a tacit possibility on a non-
church-connected campus can be an explicit goal on a church-
related campus, and the difference between the tacit and the
explicit could be decisive.

A Heritage of Human Concern

The Christian church and agencies associated with it have
traditionally demonstrated a concern for persons and for
society. The scriptural injunctions to bring nourishment to
the hungry, release to the captive, and sight to the blind, have
been translated into varieties of personal and social expression. On the college campus this human concern can have
both internal and external references. *Internally* it affects the
style and spirit of community life; *externally* it determines
the community outreach into surrounding areas of need.

The question of the degree to which it is appropriate for
academic communities to assume larger responsibilities for
personal sensitivity and psychological climate has been a
subject of long and heated argument, and it is not our objective here to retrace the battle. I share the perspective of those
who believe that the process of intellectual growth, which
is the university's first objective, is greatly enhanced if it takes
place within a context of a broad range of experiences beyond
the strictly intellectual. The university today is called to a
larger task than that of providing "the discipline and furniture
of the mind; expanding its powers and storing it with knowledge," as was suggested by the Yale faculty report of 1828.

The compendium *The American College—A Psychological*

and Social Interpretation of the Higher Learning,[5] containing
nearly thirty studies by as many authors, is indicative of a
current trend to give studied attention to the personality of
students and teachers, to the cultural situation in which they
reside on campus, to the manifold and complex dynamics
that occur in interpersonal relationships among students and
between them and their teachers, and to the bearing of all this
on the educative process. The predominant assumption of
these studies is that education is properly concerned not only
with informing minds but with changing persons.

Admittedly, such a goal is not unrelated to that sought in
psychotherapy. Sanford makes this explicit:

> Colleges are in a position to bring about, and sometimes they do
> bring about, by means that are strictly educational, changes as
> profound as those commonly wrought by psychotherapy. The
> student entering college is in important respects like the patient
> or client whom the psychotherapist welcomes most heartily;
> both the student and the promising patient exhibit a "condition"
> that cries out for change, and both reveal a heartening poten-
> tial for change.[6]

To observe that education and psychotherapy have something in common is by no means to reduce education to a kind
of therapy or make of a university a mental health clinic. To
suggest, as at least one educator has, that the two basic
processes of good education are "knowing and loving"[7] is to
risk caricature and sentimentalization. But if the university
looks at this world and its needs steadily and whole it must
ask if the indicated needs are not for something more than
sharper minds and additional information, as great as these
needs are; it must ask if the changes called for by our society
are not of the order that will be brought about ultimately by
changed persons.

The problem of poverty, for example, is not essentially a

[5] Nevitt Sanford, ed.
[6] *Ibid.*, p. 22.
[7] R. J. Havighurst, "The Emotional Outcome of General Education" in
Journal of General Education, I (1946), 39.

problem of inadequate food supply, nor do the poor health standards of most of the world arise out of inadequate human technology or understanding alone, nor are racial tensions born simply of inadequate sociological and anthropological data. Beyond the practical issues of distribution and training and factual information lie the more basic and more complex human factors of caring, imagination, sensitivity—problems that will not ultimately be solved by books, lectures, or examinations, but by caring, by imagination, and by sensitivity.

The church college bears a distinct advantage in providing this essential kind of living context. This can be attributed, in part, to its size, the majority of church-related schools being small residential colleges. A recent Carnegie Foundation report indicates that the small residential college does the best job of providing conditions which foster desirable effects in the character development of students.[8] Beyond this, there is the natural inclination toward personal concern which may be resident in the kind of person who seeks and keeps a faculty or staff position in a church college rather than moving to a larger public institution where anonymity is easier and sheer size can provide ready excuse for lack of personal attention. In faculty and staff recruitment, church colleges have in recent years laid increasing stress upon academic qualifications and teaching competence. Yet it remains true that numbers of persons qualified in these respects also possess a personal style that extends beyond sheer academic excellence. Small colleges often have a qualitative advantage over larger schools in that they are likely to attract instructors as interested in teaching as in publishing, as interested in students as in subject matter, and as interested in the entire campus enterprise as in their own particular pocket of activity.

Christians, at least some of them, have been nurtured with an appreciation for "varieties of gifts" [9] and the challenge of building an appreciation for all these gifts in society. It is

---

[8] Kenneth A. Feldman and Theodore M. Newcome, *The Impact of College on Students,* Carnegie Foundation, 1969.

[9] I Corinthians 12:4.

persons with this kind of foundation who are more likely to build bridges than fences between departments and activities and people on the campus. With a high incidence of this kind of history, a music department is less likely to say to the athletic department, "Because you cannot play Bach I have no need of you"; an athlete to the actor, "Because you cannot play Right End I have no need of you"; or the chemist to the historian, "Because you do not deal in measurable quantities I have no need of you." A concern for personal attentiveness and communal spirit is the very thing that can lend both to the discovery of a measure of integration in the proliferated campus and to an element of personal affirmation and identity—two factors that are central to the recovery of meaning and the end of irrelevance.

Human concern, in addition, has an *external* reference having to do with involvement in the larger community, the kind of conscientious involvement which we have said represents a fundamental mood of contemporary secularization, and which characterizes a university that has come of age. Again the heritage of human concern associated with the ideals of the church and its agencies contributes quite naturally to the notion of social involvement at the point of human need.

The redemptive involvement of Christians in the life of the world has historically been of two sorts: healing and transforming. There would doubtless be little question that colleges should participate to at least some degree in the healing of society, whether by cooperating with United Fund drives, encouraging students to assist the programs of local service institutions, or contributing cultural color and artistic stimulation to communities that are threatened by cultural stagnation. Little controversy will ensue from this kind of external outreach by universities.

But involvement of the other sort—participation in society as an agent of social change—though motivated by the same kind of human concern that sends students to working in orphanages, may precipitate more complex and controversial responses. If students and faculty apply the lessons learned in

political science and sociology classes to the immediate sur-
roundings of the campus in an effort to alter social structures
in the direction of maximizing human justice, the consequences for that college may be instantly disquieting.

This is one of the points at which universities confront a
challenge and face a risk not unlike those faced by churches
today. Universities, like churches, if they call their culture
into question on any but the most innocuous issues, will
sooner or later find themselves on somebody's list of un-
patriotic influences in society.

Logic would dictate that if any institution should understand both the challenge and the risk of social criticism, it is
the church-related college with its double heritage of
prophetic critique. But the implications of this mission for
any college that is dependent upon a benovolent public are
immediately apparent. At the point of this part of its responsibility, the church-related college may have to fulfill its
potential at its own peril, and the questions that arise here
concern not merely a college's responsibility, but perhaps
its very survival.

With all due attention to the factor of timing (to which
reference was made in the previous chapter), the knotty questions remain: What stance should a college take with respect
to its participation, or the participation of its constituents,
in activities that may be threatening to the college's image in
society? What does social answerability require of an academic community which is called to provide not only maximum information but also the implements for judging the
procedures and structures to which the surrounding community has become accustomed? What will be the cost of this
kind of answerability to the surrounding society? Events may
challenge a college to show its colors with respect to fundamental human issues, like poverty, racial injustice, and war.
The college may be asked to provide, let us say, for a meeting
place for a poverty march caravan, or approval for campus
participation in a "Vietnam moratorium," or a boycott of a
printer whose employment practices are questionable. All
these issues come under the heading of concern for universal

community, but any of them may generate resentment in the local community.

More often the challenge is more subtle than that of requiring the college to take an official position. The question may be whether or not a college will permit nonviolent protest to be aired on its campus for any cause at all. It may be a question of whether a college will, in spite of public misunderstanding, permit itself to be the scene of a draft information center or a draft counseling workshop. Either of these services might be provided in the name of the academic responsibility to provide information on all sides of an issue, or to challenge any social system (in spite of probable public charges of noncooperation). It may involve the question of a detailed (and perhaps uncomfortably revealing) study of the power structure of the local community (in spite of intimidating pressures on the college "to mind its own business"). The challenge of social answerability has to do, in other words, with the church college's willingness to fulfill the calling of its heritage as an instrument of human redemption, with all the risks and frustrations pertaining thereto.

The risks are not small. Most real of all are the financial hazards. A college can lose thousands of dollars in support as a result of inviting one controversial speaker to its rostrum, or it can fall into disfavor with a philanthropist because it permits open questioning of a government policy. Add to this the general "image problem" that may accrue through the years because of a university's effort to "drag its culture kicking and screaming into the twentieth century," and the result will be a business office whose task is infinitely harder than it would have been had the school not taken the deeper needs of its culture and her revolutions so seriously.

The price of social answerability can be even worse. A college may find itself in a position in which it can be true to its mission only at the expense of its life, which is to say that even with the careful application of a contextual approach to its ethical dilemma, one option that forces itself upon the scene bears a distinct resemblance to a cross. This is hardly an appealing option, to say the least. Colleges share with the rest of the human race the tendency to read past such prophetic dictums as, "What profiteth a college if it gain spectacular enrollments and magnificent endowments and lose its own integrity?"

It is all well and good, of course, for one to articulate this kind of noble ideal as long as he is not a college president or trustee. It remains true that for the man who sits on the board vested with the legal trusteeship of an institution or who occupies the position of an executor, the perspective is altogether different from that afforded the impatient student, the free-wheeling campus pastor, or the ill-informed off-campus critic. Talk as loftily as we may about how a college, particularly a church-related college, ought to be willing to sacrifice in the name of human redemption, the fact remains that there are exceedingly few presidents eager to preside over the demise of their colleges and few trustees indeed who are inclined to let it happen. The web of responsibilities which trustees and administrators bear to a concerned and supporting public is complex and involves many "triadic relationships."

Yet this is cause not to abandon the question but to sharpen it. Whereas the efforts and investments of multitudes of people are involved in decisions affecting the fate of any college, and whereas there is appeal to the argument that an imperfectly responsible college is better than no college at all, a question for each individual church-affiliated institution remains to be wrestled with to the point of an answer. The question is: If it is possible to mobilize massive moral and financial support for that college only at the expense of a serious compromise of its human heritage and spiritual task, only at the cost of its critical function at a critical time, is the college worth the sacrifice? Is any one college worth the effort of eliciting its support if it is to be simply more-of-the-same, being and doing what other colleges are being and doing? If a college cannot somehow fulfill a unique calling that is rare and crucial, would it not be wiser to merge with other colleges that are doing the customary and the mediocre? Although this is a question that ought to be put to every institution of higher learning, the church-related college has most reason of all to raise and pursue all the implications of its various alternatives. Such a school, for reason of both its freedom and its heritage, must, with every act, self-consciously weigh its potential and its peril.

Maximum Openness to Religious Considerations

Religion is by no means absent from the academic programs of state-supported institutions of higher learning. The number of credit courses in religion in state colleges is significantly greater than it was a generation ago, and the growth and development of schools of religion in state universities continues. Nevertheless, it remains true that in many areas of the country a particularly narrow interpretation of church-state separation has issued in what I call "theophobia," an almost paranoiac fear of the articulation of theology on state campuses. On some campuses ordained ministers are prohibited from making calls in dormitories. On some, public prayers are prohibited. On many campuses the programming of speakers or discussions bearing a specifically religious connotation must be relegated to locations off the campus.

Thus, on many campuses, an entire dimension of the human and intellectual reality is virtually eliminated from the educational picture. To those who believe that the open consideration of all questions, including religious ones, is essential to total human education, such restrictions cannot but be interpreted as a serious handicap to a student and a violation of academic freedom.

At this very point a church-related college enjoys a potential advantage in its ostensible openness to religious considerations on campus. Not only may this openness be expressed in terms of unshackled speakers and discussions on the campus, but in the healthy freedom of exchange in the specific area of religious questions. There is a far-reaching advantage in the tacit approval in the church-related college of spontaneous and explicit discussion of the implications of the Christian faith and of human concern. The complexity of the issues confronting the university require accessibility to every possible resource available, and exposure to every honest insight.

If prayer is anything more than a perfunctory ritual; if it is, in fact, either as a psychological exercise or a spiritual reality, a means of mobilizing one's thoughtful resources and directing them creatively, then the opening of a faculty or staff meeting with prayer can be a significant ingredient in the setting of a group mood and preparation for responsible decision-making. If there are valid insights in the biblical message which can be brought to bear upon the life style of a community, if, in other words, declaring the Word, however briefly, is an appropriate means of bringing illumination to the human situation in any context, then the Word (effectively communicated) is unquestionably valid on a campus, not only in formal services in chapel but in informal messages at faculty, trustee, or student gatherings.

Obviously there is no claim here that offering a prayer or reading a scriptural passage will automatically enhance the responsible functioning of any community. Much depends, of course, upon who is presenting the thought and how it is done. But the possibility that sharing one's deepest convictions about ultimate reality can make a difference is reason enough to employ these ancient means of expression joyfully rather than apologetically. Here the church-related college can do what the state-supported college apparently cannot do. And this privilege of unrestricted openness to religious considerations, in the fullest secular-human sense of the word, is a gift to be prized.

As every campus pastor knows, there are new means of expression and new vehicles for worship which promise far more real communication than the old reliance on words, even fresh words. As a result of this new freedom in worship, there is now more possibility of genuine worshipful experience on college campuses than there has been for many years.

Insights which have been lost in verbiage for decades are dawning afresh on hungry college youth whose religious past has left them estranged from any sense of connection with or appreciation for historical Christianity. The future in the area of ministry through popular means of expression is wide open. Posters on dormitory walls cry out for "love" and "peace." Vocalists on hit records sing of awareness and honesty. The omnipresent guitar sadly twangs behind appeals for sensitivity and sharing. The cinema gives its powerful blessing to authenticity and involvement in the world's suffering. On stages and street corners, moral courage is idealized with a fervor that would have made the commencement speaker of twenty years ago weep for joy. For what more effective teaching aids could the church ask? If the church does not, with creativity, capitalize on these assets of our generation, then it deserves to lose its connection with the college campus.

But even the gifts of relevant worship and a sense of meaningful religious heritage are not without their perils. Any community that is explicit about its religious life and open in its religious commitment runs all the customary risks of fostering new religious complacency, not to mention spiritual conceit. Aldous Huxley's warning in regard to a religiously educated bigot is pertinent: "A long religious training had not abolished or even mitigated his self-love; it had served only to provide the ego with a theological alibi. The untutored egoist merely wants what he wants. Give him a theological education, and it becomes obvious to him, it becomes axiomatic, that what he wants is what God wants." [10]

The temptations to fall victim to this kind of theological arrogance are all too common. While prayer can be a mobilizer of spiritual resources, and scriptural examination can be a guide to the mind, these can also become substitutes for authentic human action and therefore disguises for religious irresponsibility. A certain measure of protection against

[10] *The Devils of Loudun* (New York: Harper & Bros., 1952).

these perils is provided by the third potential advantage of
the church-related college:

A Theological Framework of Understanding [11]

Someone once defined a Christian statesman as one
who seeks to discern where God is planning to go over the
next fifty years. The Christian higher educator may be
defined in much the same terms. He views his task from the
perspective of faith in a God of both creation and history,
whose intentionality is at work in both nature and event, and
whose purposive action becomes the basis for faithful human
response. Christian theology need not somehow be imposed
awkwardly upon the tasks of higher education; rather, it
serves to illumine academia in a manner that can contribute
to a sense of integration, to a notion of purpose, to a consciousness of identity, to an awareness of responsibility—in
short, to a sense of meaning—throughout the many-faceted
enterprise of college life.

Referring to Jesus Christ as the incarnate Lord of creation
as well as Redeemer, in whom both processes (creativity and
redemption) are fulfilled, McCoy says:

> Jesus Christ as the logos of God becoming flesh, as the in-
> carnate Lord, may well be that central conviction of Christian
> faith by which we can understand most clearly the significance
> of higher education and the purposes and roles of colleges under
> church sponsorship. Certainly Incarnation can remind us that
> the basis of Christian decision and action in higher education as
> elsewhere is the creating, governing, redeeming action of God
> within events rather than the presence of Christians finding
> unique function in an entity vaguely designated as "secularized
> world." [12]

[11] I deal here more briefly with this consideration of "theological framework," not because it is less important than the other advantages of the
church college, but because it has been delineated so well elsewhere. Charles
S. McCoy's discussion of "Christian Faith in Higher Education" in his forthcoming book, *New Identity for the Church-Related College,* will be found
helpful to the reader, as it has been to me.

[12] *Ibid.*

To the university's task of exploring and understanding the created order, Christian theology brings the insight that creation is purposeful and intelligible, its investigation is an act of appropriate and reverent inquiry, and it is every bit as legitimate on the college campus as are Brahms and Boyle's law. To the university's task of analyzing and pursuing the critical human issues of the day, Christian theology contributes the conviction that God incarnate addresses himself to the whole world rather than to some limited part of it, and that he calls into being a community whose mission is total concern for that total world.

To the university's task of challenging and transforming its culture, Christian theology offers its prophetic tradition of divine revolution and judgment which calls man to account for his responsiveness or irresponsiveness to God's action and invitation. Christian theology beckons the university to be an answering agency.

Without jeopardizing the university's "creative diversity," without in any way imposing a comprehensive world view on the community which is destined to be pluralistic, the Christian community must witness to a prevailing concern for the well-being of universal community. Thereby, the Christian posits a focus of concern and an object of responsibility that can bring cohesion to the entire campus undertaking. It can provide a sense of ultimate interrelationship among the works of the artist, the engineer, the poet, and the politician, on campus as well as beyond it. Without endangering the essentially academic function of the university, the Christian community can provide a basis for relating the university to the surrounding world, spreading a genuine concern for all the university and all the world, and inspiring the total concern of each for the other.

The possession of such convictions about its own potential by the Christian community is always reason for gratitude, but never occasion for pride. The faith to which Christians may testify individually and collectively is reason for both jubilation of spirit and contriteness of heart. The awareness that God's instrumentality is by no means limited to Chris-

tians, that his concerns are not focused on the exclusive
well-being of the church or the college, and that his ultimate
purposes are but fractionally known by even the most perceptive among us, should give Christians every cause for caution in making absolute claims, and should arouse care in
anyone who delights in dispensing final judgments. The
measure of divinity found within the Christian movement itself will help to preserve it from the kind of conceit to which
it could easily fall victim.

The appropriate stance for Christians, as they address the
university and the world, as well as each other, is, in the
strictest Niebuhrian sense, confessional. By this we mean that
the Christian would declare his witness carefully and per-
suasively, and listen with equal precision and openness to the
witness of others. Nevertheless, declare his faith he must,
for the sharing of mature theological insights with the academic community of which he is a part can do much to dispel
the sense of irrelevance that hangs like a pall over so many
campuses.

The preceding pages (about the potentialities of the church-
related college) may seem overly idealistic when measured
against the average church school today. I have been associated with such colleges long enough to be all too aware of
their foibles and failures and of the appalling degree to
which they frequently fall short of their claims, not to mention their possibilities. The problems of inadequate leisure
time for reflection, insufficient communication, and un-
adventurous planning, of which other colleges complain, are
not noticeably different on church-related campuses where
the constituencies suffer the same human frailties and limitations that plague human beings everywhere. These are only
a few of the shortcomings with which I am painfully familiar.

Certainly there are no schools upon which the pressures
are greater than upon church colleges, and there is no reason
to anticipate that the pressures will diminish. It is not likely
that such colleges will be able to devote less time to their own
finances in the immediate future, or to the procurement of

competent faculty, or to the recruitment of talented students in the competitive market. These colleges will not be able to escape the general cry for curricular reform and instructional innovation. They dare not slacken their zeal in training youth to man the stations of the culture. But in addition to all these traditional and critical tasks rise some new and pressing responsibilities which will push colleges to the limit of their creativity and will test their moral courage and challenge their self-confidence.

Not all colleges will be a match for these contemporary challenges. Perhaps only a few will be, and these may be the ones we least expect. If so, it won't be the first time in history that the foolish have shamed the wise and the weak have embarrassed the strong. The colleges which will come of age most gracefully may be those of the most modest enrollments, who engage in intensive examination of the processes of interaction in their campus community and thereby learn skills for helping to humanize the world. They may be the colleges of the least endowment, who will risk their economic future by providing unhesitating leadership in the struggles of a crying society. They may be the colleges of the fewest federal research programs, who dare to examine carefully and constantly that theological heritage which informs and shapes their institutional purpose and their community life style.

The colleges of the future may be colleges affiliated with the church—heirs of both a great commission to dare the perilous, and a brave heritage of confidence in history. This heritage holds out a kind of freedom that could well be the envy of many an institution of higher learning that is not so free to express its full dimensionality. Hence, at the very time when some are questioning the future of the church-related college, there are reasons to believe that this very special kind of institution may well come closest to providing the needed corrective to the threat of academic meaninglessness and irrelevance of which we hear reverberation from so many quarters.

THE CHURCH'S LARGER RESPONSIBILITY

Be all this as it may, the whole hope for higher education does not lie in colleges with church connections. The church's responsibility to higher education is much larger than that. It is no longer sufficient, if it ever was, for the church to limit its concern to its own colleges or to its specific ministries on state campuses. The problems faced by institutions of higher learning are equally critical whether those institutions are supported by church, state, or private funds. And the youth whose sense of meaning is at stake are equally important to the Christian community. The internal unrest and external pressures are no less and no greater for one college than for the other. Insofar as the church concerns itself not primarily with herself and her own institutions, but with humanity and its growth and redemption, she will concern herself with higher education everywhere. This means that we should expect to find local churches rising to the defense of colleges that become the brunt of criticism born of misunderstanding. It means that we should expect to find groups of Christians lobbying for adequate budgets for state colleges. It means that we may hope to see individual Christians of the "establishment" building relationships with students, entering into dialogue with the more dissident ones and those who feel misunderstood. It means combating the easy and popular prejudices against people who look and act different from themselves. It means taking bold, creative steps to make opportunities for college youth to be *listened to* in the church and in the community. It means setting up programs to educate churchmen as to the objectives and problems of all responsible college education. It means encouraging a wide study of academic freedom and its implications. It means that a new concept of "public relations" for the campus must be developed, one that not only wins the favor of the philanthropist but creates a new image as to what a college is supposed to be.

It also means that we have reason to expect Christians to encourage colleges and universities of whatever affiliation to cultivate their "courage to be," to run the risks that today's institutions of higher learning must run in venturing out in fresh directions in academic innovation, community sensitivity, and critical social judgment. It means, in other words, that Christians on or near campuses must assist their local colleges to do, on a community level, that which they as individual selves are required to do: to confront the threats and challenges of life with daring; to spend themselves on enterprises that will outlast them and that are of ultimate value; to respond with their lives to the highest they know in order that their existence may be invested with the deepest possible meaning, and to discover creative ways of accomplishing these goals in the unique setting of their own local situation.

Although, as we said at the outset, the problems of universities must be solved chiefly by the selves who comprise them, despite the pressures of the surrounding culture, the world beyond the campus can assist immeasurably by helping to provide a social context of trust and confidence in a time when mistrust of academic communities is rampant. Encouragement is doubly helpful in areas where there is an inclination toward making of the university a safe and obedient tool of the society.

Periodically in history the church has had to master the strategies of undercover movement, not just for self-preservation, but for the purpose of initiating and supporting causes which, though they did not bear the stamp of the church, bore the identifying marks of the church's mission, or certain areas of it. The graduated income tax, women's suffrage, the care and protection of children, hospitals and homes, the labor movement, Social Security, prison reform, civil rights, humane laws, world peace, the War on Poverty, these are but a few of the causes in which the church has often lost its specific identity in order to expedite the release of captives and the recovery of sight to the blind. The cause of meaningful higher education in our time is a matter of no less priority. It is not immediately apparent that any non-Christian agency or fellowship is willing to provide this kind of massive moral and interpretive support. The Christian church, armed with the conviction that God's redeeming work is carried on both in and outside of its institutional confines, could make the vital difference in the fate of modern higher education.

INDEX